THE HAMISH HAMILTON BOOK OF MYTHS AND LEGENDS

In the same series

THE HAMISH HAMILTON
BOOK OF KINGS

THE HAMISH HAMILTON
BOOK OF QUEENS

Selected by
Eleanor Farjeon and William Mayne

THE HAMISH HAMILTON
BOOK OF PRINCES

Selected by
Christopher Sinclair-Stevenson

THE HAMISH HAMILTON
BOOK OF PRINCESSES

Selected by
Sally Patrick Johnson

THE HAMISH HAMILTON
BOOK OF WITCHES

Selected by
Jacynth Hope-Simpson

THE HAMISH HAMILTON
BOOK OF MAGICAL BEASTS

Selected by
Ruth Manning-Sanders

THE HAMISH HAMILTON
BOOK OF HEROES

Selected by
William Mayne

THE HAMISH HAMILTON
BOOK OF GOBLINS

Selected by
Alan Garner

THE HAMISH HAMILTON
BOOK OF DRAGONS

Selected by
Roger Lancelyn Green

THE HAMISH HAMILTON
BOOK OF SEA LEGENDS

Selected by
Michael Brown

THE HAMISH HAMILTON BOOK OF

MYTHS AND LEGENDS

✻◈✻◈✻◈✻◈✻◈✻◈✻◈✻◈✻◈✻◈✻◈✻

SELECTED BY

JACYNTH HOPE-SIMPSON

ILLUSTRATED BY

RAYMOND BRIGGS

HAMISH HAMILTON

LONDON

First published in Great Britain 1964
by Hamish Hamilton Ltd
90 Great Russell Street, London, WC1B 3PT
4th impression 1970
5th impression 1973

SBN 241 90231 2

PRINTED OFFSET LITHO IN GREAT BRITAIN
BY COX & WYMAN LTD,
LONDON, FAKENHAM AND READING

Contents

Introduction ix
The Flood 1
The Fight for the Crown 7
Weighed in the Balance 15
The Secret of King Minos 19
The Disgraceful Baby 31
How Winter Came to the Earth 41
The Fugitive 47
The Uninvited Guests 55
Swimming to School 73
How Thor Fooled the Giants 77
How the Giants Fooled Thor 85
The Twilight of the Gods 93
The Curse of the Dragon's Gold 101
The Water-Monsters 115
The Giant's Daughter 129
Sir Gawain and the Green Knight 145
"In You my Death, in You my Life" 163
The Werewolf 175
The Battle in the Pass 181
The Earthly Paradise 193
Sources 195

To Dermot

Introduction

THERE are so many myths and legends from all over the world that planning a book of legends felt like trying to model a figure with clay too liquid to hold any shape. In the end, to impose some shape on my material, I decided to limit the book to the myths of the civilization to which I myself, who was born in England, belong. I do not suggest that the myths of, say, China or the Americas would be any less interesting, but I felt they would be too much for the scope of one single volume. I also admit that, for me, these other myths lacked associations and undertones. This is inevitable, since they are not part of the pattern that has helped to shape my own life.

The first story in this book is about 4,000 years old and comes from what is now Iraq. The next two come from Egypt. This may seem very remote from England, but in fact English people have been reading about these ancient Middle Eastern countries for hundreds of years: in the Bible. The next stories come from Greece and Rome. These places are obviously a part of our lives today, not just because Rome once conquered us, but because Greek and Roman ideas have become a part of our thought and our art, just as their languages are a part of our vocabulary. I have included one of the most famous stories in the world, that of the Fall of Troy, and what happened to both the conquerors and defeated. Next come stories from a different race, the men of the far north, some of whom also invaded this country. Their world of ice and snow seems very far from the sunlit world of the Greeks, but they themselves were conscious of a connection. They called their gods the Aesir, or men of Asia, to show that they were descended from the heroes of Troy. I have included one story, *Beowulf*, with a Scandinavian setting which was actually written in this country in Old English. After that are two stories from what the Middle Ages called the "matter of Britain", that is the Arthurian legend. I deliberately chose two of the less familiar stories, one English and one Welsh. Then come stories from France and Germany, and finally a short extract based on the Old English version of a Latin poem about an Egyptian legend, the phoenix. In a way, this poem symbolizes the links in our civilization.

Within this range, I tried to create a variety and a balance. Some of the stories are serious and some flippant, some long, some mere anecdotes. Some of them have been used time and again by poets, musicians and painters, so that anybody who learns them in youth will recognize them, in many forms, all through his life. Others are little known. It quite often happens that myths from two or more countries have the same basic theme. In such cases I have used only one version. Sometimes the same characters appear in more than one story, but I hope that this will help to establish them as personalities. For this reason, I have used only one form of any name, for example Odysseus.

I was determined to tell these stories from early versions and to avoid consulting modern re-tellings. (Now I have finished the book I can have the pleasure of reading these.) In the case of classical myths it is easy enough to find where the story comes from, with some others it called for a certain amount of detective work. A list of sources appears at the back of the book. They are all early but, as in the case of Ovid, not necessarily the earliest. Where I could, I checked a translation with the original language, but some of the works were in languages I do not know. In these cases I was careful to avoid taking any phrases from the translation. I was especially grateful for the Loeb Classical Library and the Penguin Classics.

The other important question was how to handle the stories. I left out what struck me as downright dull. I also left out detailed descriptions of physical brutality, but tried not to disguise the fact that brutality sometimes takes place. Otherwise, I made as few alterations as possible. For anyone interested, these are the main changes. The one place where I added anything was in "The Secret of King Minos", where the original was very brief. In "The Water Monsters" I placed the fight in the cave behind the waterfall. This detail actually comes from the *Grettissaga*, which has points of resemblance with *Beowulf*. I used it because the topography of *Beowulf* itself is not always entirely clear. In "The Giant's Daughter" I shortened the list of tasks set by the giant to correspond with the list that was accomplished. I have generally used the common English form of proper names. This has sometimes, as with names from the *Eddas*, meant not following the exact usage of the originals. I have also used some descriptive names, such as the Nurse, rather than Eurycleia, to make minor characters easier to remember.

Underlying everything was the question of personal taste. I chose stories I liked, and tried to show why I liked them.

The Flood

The Flood

Gilgamesh, the great king, was very frightened of death. He knew that only one man, Utanapishtim, was immortal. After a long and difficult search he found Utanapishtim and asked him how he had gained everlasting life. This is Utanapishtim's story.

"YOU know the city of Shurrapak on the banks of the river Euphrates? Once it grew very large. It teemed with people, and the people made so much noise, like the bellowing of wild bulls, that the gods were kept awake at night. They grew tired and angry from lack of sleep, and discussed what they could do. The best thing, they decided, would be to send a flood to drown all these rowdy people.

"But one of the gods, Ea, felt friendly towards me. He came one night, while I was asleep, and whispered outside my house which was built of reeds. 'Pull down this house of yours and build a boat instead. Make her as wide as she is long, and give her a roof to cover the deck as the sky covers the earth. Then take the young of all living creatures into the boat with you.' I heard his words as if in a dream.

"As soon as it was light, I gathered my household round

me and told them what we were to do. We set to work. It took seven days to build the boat, which was very large. She had seven decks, each of them divided into nine compartments. While we were building the boat, we were busy laying in stores as well. I killed cattle and sheep to give everyone plenty to eat, and I gave wine to the workmen as freely as if it was river water. On the seventh day, we had finished.

"Then we launched the boat. I loaded her with all the gold I possessed, with my family and relations, with animals, both wild ones and tame, and the craftsmen who had helped build her. She floated in the river, so heavily laden that two-thirds of her was under the water-line. It was already starting to rain, so I battened the roof down over our heads.

"Early next morning, a black cloud charged across the sky. The land was suddenly lit up by vivid lightning, then it was plunged into blackness again. Rain came crashing down from the sky. For a moment, everybody on earth was filled with hopeless despair. Then the god of thunder smashed and shattered everything in the world, like a man wantonly smashing a cup. The storm poured over the land as enemy troops pour into a conquered country. The gods themselves were terrified at the flood. They crouched down behind the walls of heaven like dogs that have been whipped. When they peered out and saw all the drowned people floating like fish-spawn on the sea, they cried out and lamented at the sight of what they had done.

"The storm raged for six days and nights. The winds and waves fought against each other like armies in battle. On the seventh day, the winds dropped. There was silence everywhere, for everybody was dead. The sea was now as smooth as a flat roof. I opened a hatch and looked out. All around me was water, and I could not see land anywhere.

"At last, the boat drifted towards a mountain called Nisir

and grounded there. We stayed there for six days. On the seventh, I sent out a dove, but she came back because she could not find anywhere to rest. Then I sent out a swallow, but she too returned. Last, I sent out a raven. By now, the waters were going down. She found herself something to eat, then she flew off and never came back. I threw open the roof of my boat, and felt the wind and air round me once again. Then I stepped out on to the mountain top, and made a sacrifice to the gods. I burnt cedar and myrtle, and poured out a libation.

"When the gods smelt the fragrant woods burning, they came clustering round like flies. One of them was angry to see that I had escaped.

" 'We did not want anyone to survive the flood!' he exclaimed.

"But Ea, the god who had warned me, said, 'I wish that this flood had never happened. I would rather mankind had been preyed on by lions or wolves, or wasted by famine or pestilence. It was not I who warned this man. He learnt of the flood in a dream.'

"Then the gods took me and my wife away to live by the edge of the sea, remote from all other men who might come after us. Because we were the only ones to have survived the flood, they gave us eternal life."

At the end of this story Gilgamesh felt very sad. He knew now that he could never escape death himself. He set off to return to his own city. But Utanapishtim's wife felt sorry for him, and persuaded her husband to tell him a secret. If he would dive deep into the sea he could bring up a magic plant which would make him eternally young. He did so, but instead of eating the plant straight away, he decided to take it back home to share with the people there. While he was bathing at a water-hole, a serpent seized the plant and ate it. At once it cast off its old skin and appeared in a shining new one. Now Gilgamesh had lost his last chance of immortality. He returned home. There he governed his people wisely and justly. He had an account of all he had seen and heard written down on clay tablets. This is how we know the story of the great flood. In due course he died, but his story survived, and so, after all, he became in one sense, immortal.

The Fight for the Crown

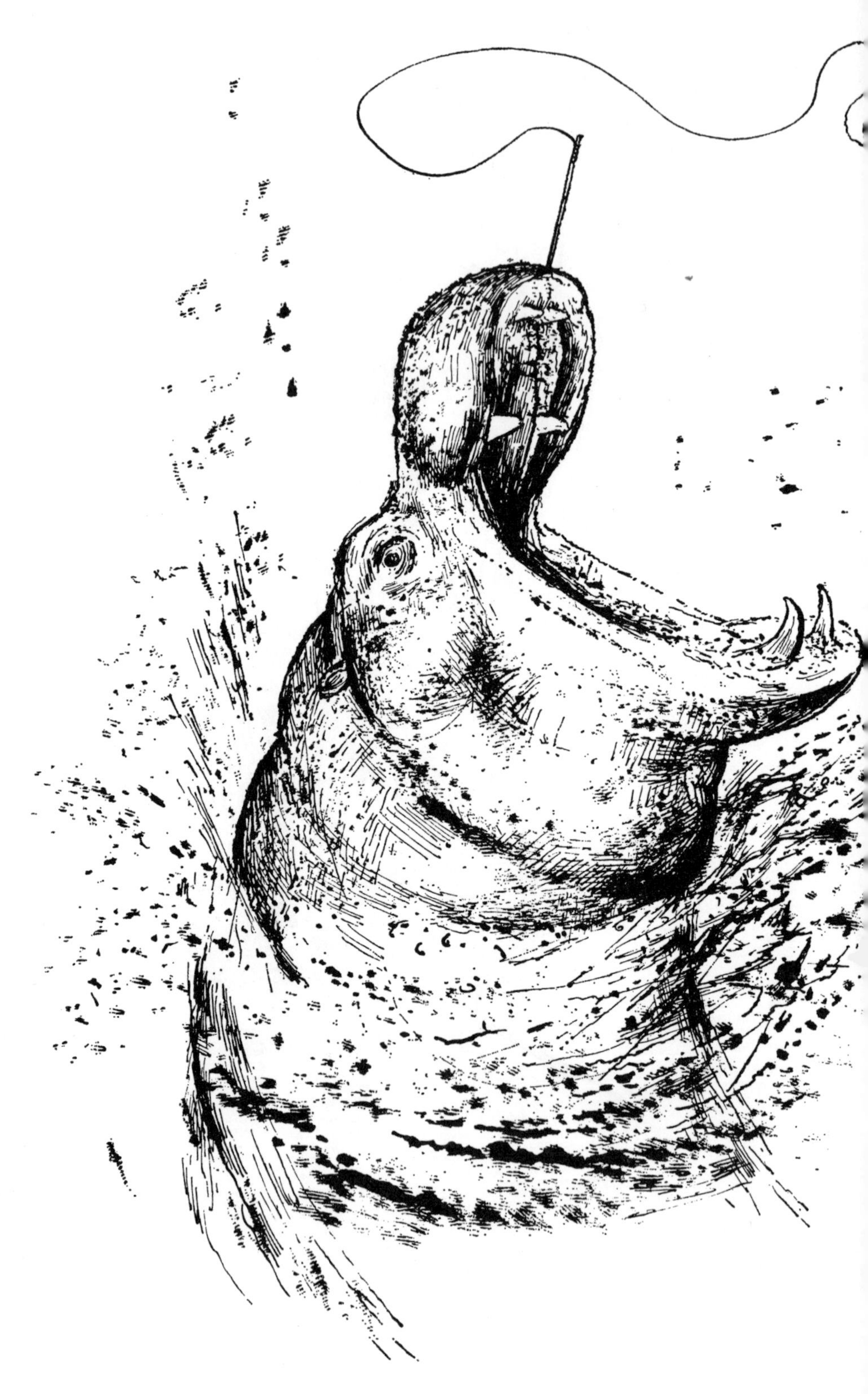

The Fight for the Crown

ONE of the bitterest quarrels the gods ever had was about the great White Crown of the god Osiris.

Osiris himself was killed by his evil brother, Set. Osiris's wife, Isis, escaped to the swamps of the Nile delta. There she hid in the reeds with her baby son, Horus, so that Set could not kill them as well. When Horus grew up, he wished to avenge his father. He thought that he, and nobody else, should sit on Osiris's throne and wear his crown. So began the struggle.

First Horus petitioned the god Ra, lord of all, to give him the crown. Several other gods and goddesses supported him. This only angered Ra, who thought it was up to him to decide, not all those whippersnappers of minor gods. In any case, he wanted Set to have Osiris's throne because he was older and stronger than Horus. So they argued for eighty years. In the end, Thoth, the god of justice, wrote to the Mother of the Gods to see if she could solve their difficulty.

"Let Horus have his father's crown," she wrote back. "But double Set's property for a consolation, and let him have both your daughters for extra wives."

Thoth read the letter aloud to the gods who became very excited.

"Give Horus the crown," they shouted.

This made Ra obstinate.

"Horus is young and weak," he objected.

At this the gods shouted angrily, and one of them, Baba, started to jeer at Ra.

"You're hopelessly out of date. People don't worship you any longer."

Most of the gods thought Baba had gone too far, but Ra was deeply offended. He lay down on his back and sulked for the rest of the day. In the end, the gods decided to go to an island a little distance away. They hoped that once there they could discuss the problem in peace and calm. Even so, there were difficulties.

"Isis may come," grumbled Set. "She's determined to get the crown for that son of hers, and she's quite unscrupulous."

"That's easy enough," Ra replied. "Just warn Anty the ferryman not to take her across."

So they all went across to the island. Isis waited until they were safely out of the way. Then she disguised herself as an old woman, and hobbled along to see Anty the ferryman.

"Please take me across. I've got to take food to a little boy who is looking after the cattle on the island. He's been over there for five days, and will be hungry by now."

"The gods warned me I wasn't to take any woman across."

"That's different. They meant Isis. Isis the beautiful young goddess! They didn't mean someone like me."

"What will you give me?" asked Anty.

"Some of the bread I've got for the little boy."

Anty shook his head.

"Nothing doing."

"Very well. I'll give you a gold ring."

So Anty took her across. As soon as she was safely on the island, she changed herself into a very beautiful girl. She sauntered about by the pavilion where all the gods were having a meal. As she had hoped, Set caught sight of her. He slipped away from the other gods, and hid behind a bush.

"Come and stay with me for a little," he called in beguiling tones.

Isis approached him, with her eyes modestly on the ground. She even managed to blush a little.

"Oh, my great lord," she said meekly. "I am the widow of a poor shepherd. Please can you help my son? A stranger has come and taken his father's cattle away from him."

"That's disgraceful!" said Set. "You can't take a man's property away from his rightful heir."

He was full of indignation that this pretty girl had been badly treated, and saw himself as a strong man protecting her. For a moment, he did not realize how she had tricked him. Then suddenly Isis changed herself into a bird. She flew to the top of the tree, and started to taunt him.

"There! You've condemned yourself. You've said that you shouldn't take a man's property away from his son. What do you think that you're doing to my poor Horus?"

Set burst into tears. He went back and told Ra about it, crying the whole time. Ra was unsympathetic.

"It's all your own fault. You can't do anything now."

They all went back home again, and Ra ordered the gods to give Horus the great White Crown of his father Osiris. When they delayed, Ra was very angry, as though it had been he all along who had wanted to give Horus the crown. At last, they began to crown Horus, and Set raised a shriek of protest.

"I'm just not standing for this! Take that crown off him at once. Let's have a proper fight to decide who's going to have it."

Ra changed his mind yet again.

"That's a good idea. It would really settle the matter."

Set followed up his advantage.

"Suppose we both change into hippopotamuses. We'll dive into the water, and if either of us comes up to breathe before three months is over, he will have lost the crown."

They both disappeared under the water. Isis sat down on the edge and cried.

"I don't trust Set in the least. I'm sure he will try to hurt Horus."

In an effort to help her son, she tied a harpoon to a rope and hurled it into the water to try to kill Set. She hit Horus instead.

"Help!" shouted Horus in pain.

Isis hauled out the harpoon. She was determined not to be beaten and hurled it straight in again. This time it hit Set.

"Help! Help!" he shrieked loudly.

He made so much noise that Isis, not really thinking what she was going, pulled out the harpoon again in order to make him quiet. Horus shot up to the surface. He was spluttering, and looked very angry with Isis.

"Mother, this is intolerable. You're just making a fool of me."

So they went on and on, behaving not like two gods but like a couple of spoilt children. They had a boat race, and agreed that the winner should have the crown. Set's boat sank, so he promptly turned himself into a hippopotamus and tried to tip Horus into the water as well. The other gods got thoroughly tired of them both.

"We can't stand any more fights, Set. You must decide the

matter legally," said Ra. This was at least the fourth time he had changed his mind. In the end, Set gave in, and agreed that Horus should have the White Crown and should sit on the throne of his father, Osiris. As a compensation, Ra made Set the god of the storm. This was a most appropriate choice, for it gave Set a chance to be destructive and violent, and to make as much noise as even he wanted to.

Weighed in the Balance

Weighed in the Balance

AFTER a man dies, he has to set out on a very dangerous journey. First he must cross a wild and very difficult country, where devils and fiends and evil spirits live. Savage beasts, such as crocodiles, will try to destroy him. His only hope of safety is to carry the right amulets or charms, and to know the right spells to say. At last, he will reach the Hall of Judgement, where the god Osiris and forty-two judges will decide if he is worthy of everlasting life. Here, he must justify his behaviour on earth. He must persuade his judges that he has done no evil, that he has not murdered or blasphemed, stolen from his neighbour or given false measure.

After this, his heart will be taken out and weighed in the balance. The heart is put on to one pan of the scales, and the goddess of Truth, or else a feather which is her symbol, is put in the other. The god Thoth will check the weight and record it. If the two sides weigh exactly the same, it will be proof that he was a just man while he lived on earth, and he will be allowed to mix freely with the gods and the spirits of other dead men. If the balance does not weigh evenly, his heart will be snapped up by a monster which waits crouched behind Thoth. This monster is part lion, part hippopotamus, part crocodile, and is called the Devourer of the Dead.

The Secret of King Minos

The Secret of King Minos

KING MINOS of Crete lived in the most beautiful palace in all the world. It was very large, so large that you could lose yourself in it quite easily. The walls were covered with paintings of octopuses and dolphins, so that sometimes you felt as if you were walking under the sea. The palace was very cheerful with sounds of feasts and music and dancing, but sometimes at night, when the music had stopped, a terrible roar would come up from the very depths of the earth. Everybody would shudder and hide their faces. They would whisper to one another, "It is the Minotaur."

The Minotaur was a very terrible creature. It lived in an underground maze, far underneath the palace. Nobody knew what it looked like. Nobody dared to talk about it out loud. The only person who ever saw it was King Minos himself. At night he would creep down to the labyrinth where the terrible monster lived. He would play with it and fondle it. A few brave people whispered to one another that Minos loved it more than he loved his own daughter. They knew he would give it anything that it wanted.

Every spring, King Minos would send a message to King Aegeus of Athens who lived far away, over the sea. The message was always the same.

It said, THE MINOTAUR IS HUNGRY. SEND ME SEVEN YOUNG MEN AND SEVEN BEAUTIFUL GIRLS AND I WILL GIVE THEM TO HIM TO EAT. IF YOU DO NOT, I WILL COME WITH MY SHIPS AND BURN DOWN YOUR CITY. I WILL KILL EVERY MAN AND WOMAN AND CHILD IN THE WHOLE OF ATHENS.

Then all the young men and girls in Athens would be gathered together and have to draw lots. The unlucky ones, on whom the lot fell, would sail away to Crete to be fed to the Minotaur. Their fathers and mothers and brothers and sisters would stand down at the harbour and watch them go. Some of them would pretend to be brave, and others would cry.

Now, King Aegeus of Athens had a son called Theseus. He was strong and brave and skilled at wrestling and fighting and throwing a spear. He was very angry that Minos should ask for this tribute, and planned what he could do to stop him.

One year, when the message came from King Minos, Theseus strode down to the market place where all the young men and women of Athens were gathered.

He said, "I will be one of the seven young men who are going to Crete. I swear I will kill the Minotaur, or else never come back alive."

So Theseus set off for Crete. The ship had dismal black sails, because all the men and women of Athens were feeling so sad. As he went on board, King Aegeus said unhappily, "Promise me, that if you come back alive, you will put white sails on the ship. I will watch for you every day, and if I see the white sails, I will know that you have killed the terrible Minotaur and are coming home safely."

They sailed on to the island of Crete. A party of Cretan soldiers met them, and marched them up to the palace of King Minos. The palace was called Cnossos.

It happened that day that Ariadne, who was King Minos's daughter, was sitting by the walls of the palace sewing. She was very happy. The sun was shining brightly, the birds sang, and all the valley before her was golden with spring flowers. She was sewing a pattern of white lilies against a bright blue sky. Then she looked up. She saw the young men and girls who were being marched up to Cnossos to be fed to the Minotaur. All at once, she felt helpless and sad.

"Why should they die?" she said to herself. "They are no older than I am. How dreadful to be fed to the Minotaur, and never to see the blue sky again."

That night she was so unhappy she could not sleep.

She got up and dressed and crept out into the huge courtyard. The night air was warm and smelt of flowers and cypress trees. Suddenly, she thought she heard someone moving. Before she could make sure, a terrible roar came up from the ground under her feet. It was the Minotaur. Someone beside her caught his breath sharply.

"Who are you?" she gasped.

A man's hand caught her wrist.

"Quiet, or I may have to kill you. Where does the Minotaur live?"

Ariadne realized who it must be. One of the young men from Athens had escaped from the guard. What was he going to do?

"The Minotaur lives in a labyrinth under the palace. You go down a secret passage to get there. Only my father is supposed to know where the entrance is. But I watched him once."

The man clutched her tightly. She felt the edge of his dagger against her neck.

"Are you King Minos's daughter?"

Ariadne just managed to stop her teeth chattering.

"Yes, who are you?"

"I am Theseus, son of King Aegeus of Athens," the young man said proudly. "I have sworn to my father that I will kill the terrible Minotaur, or else never come back alive. Now show me where he lives."

Suddenly, Ariadne knew that she wanted to help him. She hated the Minotaur, and she thought that it ought to be killed. She did not want Theseus and his companions to be sacrificed to it. She felt very sorry for Theseus, although she thought he had very bad manners.

"Take that knife of yours away from my neck, and then I'll show you," she said.

Hand in hand, they crept through the palace. Everyone was asleep. At last, they came to a tiny room, which was under the throne room of Minos.

"You lift the flagstone there in the corner," said Ariadne.

Theseus pulled and heaved until the flagstone came up. A waft of hot stuffy air blew up into their faces. They could hear the faint sound of the Minotaur champing away at its food. It sounded a long way off. Ariadne thought of the stories which she had heard whispered by palace servants.

"It's like a maze down there. There are so many twists and turnings. You might never find your way back."

She clenched her hand in her pocket, and as she did so, she touched the two balls of thread, one white and one blue, with which she had been sewing that afternoon.

"Take this with you, Theseus, and unwind it as you go. Then when you have killed the Minotaur, it will show you the way to come back. I will wait here for you and hold the end of the thread."

Theseus took it from her without speaking. Then he took down a little rush-light which burnt in a niche, and, holding this in front of him, lowered himself through the hole in the floor.

He was standing on some rough steps, which went deep down into the earth. At last he came to the bottom, and found himself standing on rock. The walls were running with damp. The air was hot and stuffy, with a strange, wild animal, jungly smell. He made himself walk along the tunnel. His feeble light shone only a few feet ahead. He forgot about his father and Ariadne, and everything else in the world, except for the Minotaur.

Soon he was gasping, because it was hard to breathe. His eyes were blinded with sweat. The passage kept on twisting and turning. He kept on coming up against a blank wall of clammy rock. Then he would have to go back to the last turn and start finding his way again. Sometimes there was absolute silence except for the slow drip of water on to the rocky floor. He felt as though he was the only man in the world.

Then he could hear noises, a snuffling, a trampling of feet. The noises were nearer and nearer. Soon, he would be in the Minotaur's secret lair. What was the terrible Minotaur like? No one, except King Minos, had ever seen him and come out alive.

He could hear the creature breathing, but its breath sounded different, slow and deliberate, drawn in through its teeth. It had sensed that someone was coming and was lying in wait.

Thesens laid his ball of thread down on the floor. There were only a few inches left, and he needed his hand for his dagger. He went forward very slowly. In his right hand he held his dagger, and in his left hand the little, flickering lamp. He wanted to see what sort of creature it was he would have to fight.

Then he saw it. The passage opened out into a rocky cave and it was standing a few feet ahead. It had huge curling horns with vicious points that were stained brown with dried blood. Its eyes were half hidden by shaggy hair. Its mouth was open to show its strong, ugly teeth.

It was a bull, thought Theseus. The dreaded monster was only a bull. A bull, he knew, had more strength than a man, but a man had the greater cunning. He might manage to kill it.

Then the Minotaur stood up. Theseus saw its body which

was covered with thick matted hair. The body was not that of a bull, but of some other creature. It stretched out its front legs, and Theseus suddenly realized that these were not legs but arms, and at the end of the arms were terrible strong, hairy hands that were going to strangle him. The Minotaur was half man.

As the Minotaur's hands touched his shoulder, Theseus dropped his lamp. He lifted his hands to try to prise its fingers away, but it was too strong for him. It was bending down over him now, and one of those cruel horns pierced the skin on his back. The dreadful stench of its hot breath made him feel dizzy. He had only one chance.

He drew back his arm, then thrust his dagger, hard, into where he thought the Minotaur's heart must be. A drop of hot blood splashed on to his hand, then the metal grated against a rib. The Minotaur stepped back, snarling.

Theseus's lamp had gone out when he dropped it, and there was no light at all. They shifted round cautiously, a few feet apart, hesitating to close with one another again. Theseus realized that he was very afraid. This creature, which he had sworn to kill, had not only the strength of a savage beast, but the skill of a man as well.

The Minotaur sprang, and Theseus's knife grazed its shoulder. They separated, then started to pace round in the darkness, each waiting for the best moment to close and kill. Only their quick, harsh breathing, and the faint shuffle of feet on the rocky ground, betrayed where they were.

Then the Minotaur sprang again, and, this time, Theseus leapt. He seized hold of the monster's horns where they grew out of the shaggy hair, and leapt on to its crouched shoulders. It tried to haul him off, but he was feeling desperately for a soft spot in its neck where he could thrust in his dagger. He found one, and dug deep in. The Minotaur became frenzied, trying to throw him off in a wild dance of death, until, at last, it became more and more feeble and sank down on the floor. Theseus lay there astride it, until its breathing had stopped.

Theseus lay sprawled on the floor for one moment. He wanted to go to sleep. He could lie there, in that terrible room, hot with the smell of the Minotaur's newly-shed blood, and never wake up again. He made himself get up, and started to crawl forward on hands and knees, because he was too weak to stand. He did not know how to find his way out in the dark.

Almost by accident, he touched Ariadne's thread which he had forgotten. He started to follow it back to the light and air. He lost count of time. When he reached the knot he had made between the two balls of thread, he knew he was getting nearer. He rested there for a moment, and then made himself go on again. At last, he crawled up the steps into the little room. He stood up, staggering helplessly. He gasped at the cool, fresh air, and dragged it into his lungs.

A girl was standing there. He knew, vaguely, that it was Ariadne.

"Come on," she urged. "It is nearly light. There is no time to waste."

She pulled him upstairs, and into the palace courtyard. The sky was a pale, dull grey. They crept out through a little gate in the walls.

"We will go to the harbour," said Theseus. "My companions have already escaped and gone back to the ship from Athens."

They sailed away from Crete as the dawn turned the sky into rose-colour and gold. The sailors rigged an awning on deck for Theseus, and he lay there and slept, exhausted. Sometimes he would sigh in his sleep and shudder, as in his dreams he remembered the dreadful dark cave, and the feeling of the monster's hot breath on his neck.

He slept on and on. Occasionally he woke, and would drink or walk a few paces on deck, but he always had the dazed look of a man who does not know what he is doing. Then he would sink back on his pallet and sleep again. Once they stopped at the island of Naxos. Ariadne wandered ashore to pick wild flowers. The sailors grew anxious, for they saw a storm coming. They wanted to get away from the dangerous rocky coast, and out to the open sea. As the storm clouds grew nearer, they set sail again.

The first squall of rain hit them. The cold water fell on Theseus's cheek and woke him. For the first time for days, his head was perfectly clear.

"Where is the princess of Crete?" he asked one of the sailors.

The man looked horrified. They had been so anxious to get away from Naxos before the storm, that they had forgotten about her, and left her there on the island.

"We must go back," Theseus said.

As he spoke, he knew it was hopeless. The ship rode on and on, before the worst of the storm. If they turned back, the ship might be hurled on to the sharp reefs of rock around Naxos. The merciless sea would batter it into pieces, and they would all be drowned.

At last, the storm died down. They were approaching Athens. Theseus kept on wondering what had happened to Ariadne. All he had to remind him of her was a little tangle of blue and white thread.

All this time, King Aegeus was watching from a high cliff near Athens to see if his son would come back. At last, he caught sight of the ship in which Theseus had set sail. He strained his eyes to see what colour the sails were. If they were white, he would know that Theseus had come back safely. They were still black. Theseus must be dead. He took one step forward in order to see more clearly. Perhaps he was wrong after all. His feet slipped and he fell forward into space, then slipped down and down, to be drowned in the surging water below.

Theseus had forgotten the promise he had made to his father, that if he came home safely he would put white sails on his ship. All the things that had happened had put it out of his mind.

As he stepped ashore, he was hailed as the new king of Athens. Everyone praised him for killing the Minotaur. They feasted and rejoiced. Never again would young men and girls have to sail to Crete to be fed to the terrible monster.

Only Theseus was sad, because of the death of his father. He proclaimed that the sea in which Aegeus was drowned should be called the Aegean, so that everyone would remember his father's name.

He was so busy governing Athens, that he almost forgot Ariadne. Sometimes the girl whom he had met in the darkness at Cnossos seemed like a dream. He was not even sure what she looked like. Years later, he heard a story that she had given birth to a child on Naxos, and that the child was his. Then seafarers told him another story, that Dionysus, the god of wine, had found her on Naxos and made her his wife. He never knew the truth of what had happened to her, and nobody knows to this day.

The Disgraceful Baby

The Disgraceful Baby

WHEN Zeus, the greatest of all the gods, and the goddess Maia had a son, he could not be expected to be like ordinary children. In fact, everyone soon admitted that there had never been a baby like Hermes before, which was just as well.

Hermes was born at dawn. His mother wrapped him up carefully, and laid him to sleep in a cradle. She put the cradle inside the mouth of a cave, so that he would not get burnt by the midday sun. Then she left him for a little. He looked so sweet and innocent, she thought, that nobody could possibly want to harm him.

For a few minutes after she left, Hermes lay back in his cradle and gurgled and sucked his thumb. That was the way that a baby ought to behave. Then he got tired of behaving properly. He felt bored. He wriggled out of his cradle, and managed to stand up. After a bit of practice, he found he could walk a few steps. He wobbled out of the cave. The first thing he saw was a large tortoise. He gave a cry of delight.

"Come and play with me, tortoise," he said. "Come back to my cave."

He swooped down and picked up the tortoise. It was nearly as heavy as he was. He hugged it tight and staggered back to the cave. Then he killed the tortoise with one blow, and scooped out the flesh from the shell. He made holes all round the edge, and strung reeds across it. He plucked them, and musical notes came out. Hermes started to sing. It was a most scandalous song, which made fun of his parents. For a little while he was happy, trying to think of something really shocking to say.

Then he had another idea. He was hungry. If his mother came back, she would give him milk. What use was baby stuff like milk to a boy like him? He wanted a proper meal, something solid and tasty. Supposing he found some oxen to kill? This would need working out. He sat down to think hard.

He knew that Apollo, the sun god, kept oxen grazing nearby. He could probably drive them away. But their tracks would lead straight back to the cave, and everyone would be able to find out who the thief was. He would have to disguise his tracks. He played a few chords on his tortoise-shell lyre, and made up a very rude poem about his mother's cook. Then he had an inspiration. He cut some twigs from a tamarisk shrub, and plaited them into what looked like snowshoes. With those on his feet, nobody would recognize his footsteps. He waddled out of the cave with his large shoes flapping. He made straight for where Apollo kept his oxen and only stopped once. That was to tell an old man who was tending his vines that he did not know the right way to do it. There was no doubt that Hermes was a very naughty baby indeed.

When he reached the oxen, he started to drive them away. Their feet made very clear tracks in the sandy soil, so he drove them round and round for a bit, and finally made them walk backwards. That ought to muddle anybody, he thought. He drove them along with a little stick, swishing hard at their legs, for he could not reach any higher. He was so tiny, being a baby, that he could walk straight underneath them without having to duck down at all.

When he reached a place where no one would interrupt him, Hermes made a huge pile of wood. He took two sticks and rubbed them hard together. At first, nothing happened. Hermes was not to be thwarted like that. He rubbed harder still, scowling all the time, and, at last, they burst into flame. He hastily lit the fire. Now for the real business. It is very hard work for a baby to kill an ox, which is a massive creature, but cunning Hermes managed to trip two of them up and to kill them both on the ground. He dragged them across to the fire and started to roast them. It was very hard work indeed, but all the same, Hermes was having a wonderful time.

The roasting meat smelt good, and his mouth filled with saliva. Then a faint twinge of conscience nagged him. Was this really the way for a baby god to behave? Perhaps he should do something to show what a kind, noble, unselfish baby he really was. He would lay out the roast oxen as a sacrifice to the other gods. What a very good baby, he thought. He even tidied up after himself, which most babies would not have bothered to do. He toddled back to his cave, and got into his cradle again. He was glad to see that his lyre was still safe, so he cuddled it with one hand, and played with the bedclothes with the other. How pretty and innocent he must look.

Just then, his mother came in.

"What have you been up to, Hermes?" she said severely.

"Coo, coo, glug, glug," answered baby Hermes. He blew a few bubbles in what he hoped was a very beguiling way.

"It's no use pretending, Hermes," his mother replied.

"Apollo is very cross. He is going to come and tie you up, so you can't do any more mischief."

Hermes gave her his sweetest smile.

"Very well, Mother. We both know that I'm not like other babies, so we might as well admit it. Don't worry about Apollo. I'll get the better of him."

Meanwhile, Apollo, who was very angry indeed, was trying to find out who had stolen his oxen. The only person whom he could find to ask was the old man tilling his vineyard. At first he simply said, "Er" and "Ar", and would not answer Apollo's questions at all.

"You must know if you saw anybody or not," Apollo said crossly.

"If I was to tell you, you wouldn't credit it," said the old man. He spat. "What I thought I saw was a baby. A little thing, that couldn't have been born more than a week. He was driving those oxen of yours along, and, to make things worse, they seemed to be going backwards. If I was to tell my old woman, she'd say I was drunk."

Apollo hurried off. He followed the tracks. What a muddle they were, he thought. And what were those extraordinary footprints, so large and such a strange shape? There was no living creature, not a wolf or a bear or a lion, that had feet as immense as that. What if baby Hermes had been up to something? Trust Zeus to have that sort of son! He hurried off to the cave.

When he got there, the baby was lying in his cradle, hugging his precious lyre. He peeped out at Apollo, above the top of the bed-clothes, and gave him a very sweet smile.

"What have you done with my oxen?" Apollo demanded fiercely.

"What oxen?" asked baby Hermes.

"Tell me quickly, you little rogue, or I'll hurl you down to the Underworld, and you'll never be able to come back to the daylight again."

Hermes opened his eyes as wide as he could, then he shut them and sighed.

"I can't think what you're talking about. You need to be really big and strong to steal oxen. Here am I, a poor innocent baby. All I can do is to sleep and drink milk, or kick my bed-clothes around a bit, and have a nice warm bath. If you spread the story around that I stole your oxen, all the other gods will just laugh at you. Why, think of my poor baby feet. The skin's much too soft for me to go walking on horrible rough roads. I never heard such a story."

He screwed up his face, and whistled.

"Don't think you'll get away with it, you young rascal," Apollo said. He scooped the baby up from his cradle.

"What are you going to do with me?" Hermes protested. "Why, I don't even know what oxen look like. I wish I had never heard of them, if this is the sort of thing that is going to happen to me."

"I'm not having any more of this nonsense," Apollo growled. "Let's go and see what Zeus has to say."

He carted the baby, now sobbing and rubbing his eyes, off to Mount Olympus. Zeus, the greatest of all the gods, was sitting there, having a rest.

"What are you doing with that little creature?" yawned Zeus. He had forgotten for the moment that Hermes was his own son. "Why do you come bothering me, the greatest of all the gods, when it's obvious that I'm busy?"

"Because it's important," Apollo snapped. "This baby here, he's the wickedest, most treacherous child that's ever been born. Believe it or not, he stole my oxen. He drove them backwards, to try to muddle me up when I followed their tracks. And as for the tracks that he left himself, I've never seen anything like them. I can't even begin to think how he made them. Luckily for me, somebody saw him at it. So I followed his tracks, and found that he'd killed my oxen and scattered the ashes. Then the little wretch crept back to his cave and got into his cradle. When I arrived, he was cooing away and swearing that he didn't even so much as know what an ox was."

Baby Hermes sighed deeply.

"Here I am, Zeus, a helpless, new-born creature, that's never had time to tell a lie in my life. Listen to how he's bullying me! Do I look strong enough to steal anyone's oxen? Please, dearest Father, for after all that's what you are, help a poor little innocent baby."

With that, he winked at his father.

Zeus burst out laughing. He had no illusions at all as to what his son was really like.

Then he said in a dignified tone, "I'm not going to do anything for the moment. I think you two had better go and inspect the scene of the crime, and see if you can reach an agreement. Apollo, you're not to bully, and, Hermes, you just try and tell the truth for a change."

So Apollo and Hermes went back, and Hermes showed Apollo where he had killed two oxen. The rest were hidden away in a cave, so he drove them out.

"I can't think how you did it," Apollo said. "And I dread to think what you'll be like when you're a bit bigger. I'll have to do something about you, or you'll never stop plaguing the gods."

With that, he cut some flexible twigs and tied Hermes' hands together. Hermes just wriggled his hands, and the twigs sprang open again. He ran off to try to find somewhere to hide. Then he had a better idea. He took up his lyre, which he had been clutching all this time, and started to sing to its music. It was a different sort of song from his usual ones, very beautiful, very poetic, all about how the world was made. Apollo was deeply moved.

"You are the most wonderful baby that's ever been born," he sighed.

So from that day, Apollo and Hermes became the closest of friends, and Hermes helped to look after Apollo's oxen. Apollo did not quite trust Hermes, however, so he made him promise never to rob him again. Hermes kept his promise. Whenever he wanted to do something else really wicked, and this happened quite often, he did it to somebody else.

How Winter Came to the Earth

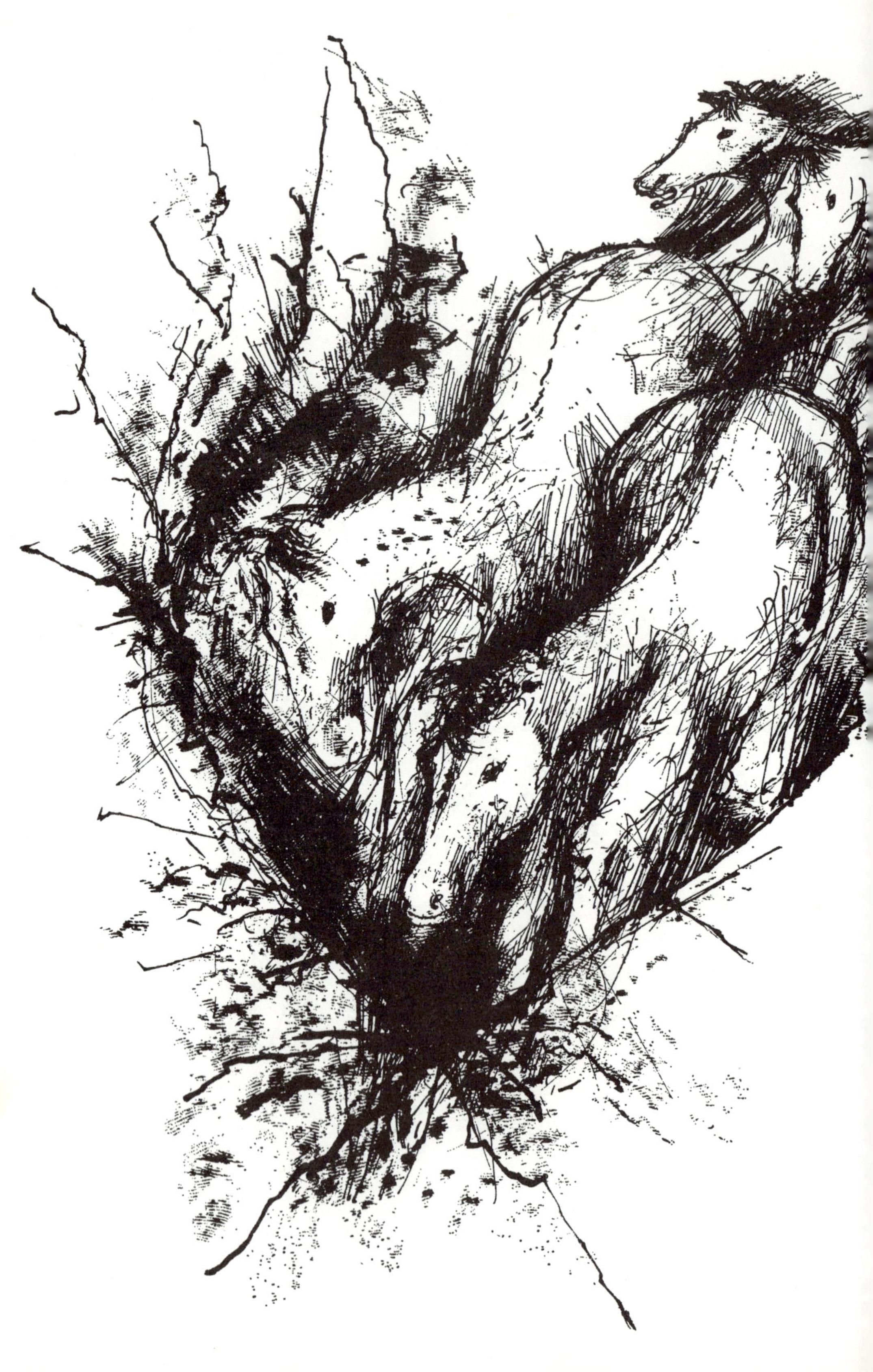

How Winter Came to the Earth

A VERY long time ago, it was always spring and summer. The flowers bloomed all the time, and the leaves never withered and died. The same trees would bear flowers and fruit at the same time. If you wanted to eat, you just plucked some fruit off the tree, and soon more fruit would ripen to take its place. The meadows were always golden and rich with corn. As soon as the reapers cut it down with their sickles, tender new shoots would begin to appear through the earth. The goddess of the spring and summer and harvest was called Demeter. She had golden hair, the colour of corn when the sun shines on it, and she was always as peaceful and calm as a long summer's afternoon. She had one daughter called Persephone, whom she loved more than anything else in the world.

One afternoon, Persephone and her friends were picking flowers at a place called Enna in the island of Sicily. They were in the shade of a wood, for the sun was only just past its highest. The sound of a little waterfall, gently splashing, made the air seem cool and fresh. Persephone was picking the white lilies which grew there all the year round. She was so anxious to pick more flowers than any of her friends, that, when her basket was full, she began to put the flowers in the front of her dress. Then she spotted a place where the lilies seemed to grow more thickly than anywhere else. She wandered a little away from her friends. She had no idea that she was being watched.

As she moved away from her friends, the man who was watching her, followed. He drove his chariot cautiously, half-hidden by the shade of the trees. It was Hades, king of the Underworld. He had seen Persephone in the distance and fallen in love with her. Suddenly, he lashed his horses on and drove swiftly towards her. She spun round to see what the noise was. As she did so, he leant over the edge of his chariot and dragged her into it. Her dress was torn and the flowers fell out. Despite the plight she was in, she cried out at losing them. She was so used to being treated kindly, that at first it never occurred to her that he meant to steal her away.

He urged his horses on. He called on each one by name, and shook the dark reins that lay on their necks. The chariot sped away from the cool, sweet-smelling woods, into a rocky land, where boiling water bubbled up from the earth and the pools reeked of sulphur. Persephone shrieked for her friends and her mother, but mostly for her mother. Suddenly Hades smote the earth and a deep gash appeared. The chariot rushed down it, towards the hidden Underworld, where Hades was king.

When Demeter heard that her daughter had disappeared, she swore that she would travel over the whole world to find her, and that she would never rest. She cut two branches of pine, and carried them up to the crater of the volcano, Etna. There she lit them, so that their flame would show her the way on her journey. She walked all day, and all night, and all the next night as well. Nobody would have recognized her. Her golden hair, which had been so shining and smooth, now hung lankly over her face, because she had torn at it in her grief. Her eyes, which had been so joyful and calm, were wild. She stopped at a little hut for a drink, and an old woman gave her some barley water. A boy, who was watching her, mocked her, because she looked nearly insane. She threw the dregs of her drink at him, and he turned into a lizard. She wept and was astonished at what she had done.

It would take too long to tell about everywhere that she went to look for her daughter. She did not stop until there was nowhere left in the whole world. Then, at last, she came back to Sicily. There she found Persephone's girdle still floating on a pool, near where she had disappeared into the earth. At the sight of it, Demeter became as wild with grief as if she had only just learnt that her daughter had disappeared. She began to curse the whole of the world, and especially Sicily. She snatched up the farmers' ploughs and smashed them. She laid fierce curses on the land. Now the crops died as soon as they pushed through the earth. If they survived, the heat shrivelled them up, or the cold wind blasted them, or floods washed them away. Birds swooped down and ate up the seeds, as the farmer was scattering them. Weeds choked all the flowers.

Then the fountain-nymph, Arethusa, said, "Demeter, be merciful to the land. I can tell you where Persephone is. I saw her with my own eyes, as I was gliding along the underground river, Styx. She has become the queen of the Underworld. She looked very sad, but she had the air of a queen."

When Demeter heard this, she grew frenzied with grief again. When at last she became more calm, she decided to go to heaven to see Zeus, the greatest of all the gods. She implored him to help her, and Zeus at last agreed.

"You can have Persephone back on one condition," he said. "If she has let any food pass her lips while she was in the Underworld, she will have to stay there forever."

Now, Persephone had been so sad in the Underworld that she had never eaten. Hades had tried to tempt her with fine and elaborate food, but she had always pushed it away. Then, one day, she had walked under a pomegranate tree. She had seen the fruit hanging down like little red lanterns. It had reminded her of the happy times when she had gathered the ripe harvest on earth, and so she had picked one pomegranate. She had peeled off the thick skin and chewed at the seeds, which are the edible part of this fruit. She had eaten seven. Nobody would have seen her, if a boy called Ascalaphus, who was working in the garden, had not been spying on her.

Hades said he would let Persephone go, as he believed she had never eaten anything in his kingdom. But, just as she was going, Ascalaphus told him that he had seen Persephone eat the seeds. It seemed now as if she would never escape.

Then Zeus decided to pity the sorrowing mother and child. He could not release Persephone from the world underground forever, because he now knew she had eaten while she was there. So he said that she might go back to her mother for half of the year. The rest of the time, she must stay with Hades.

That is why, every spring, Persephone returns to her mother, Demeter. They laugh and rejoice. The sun shines, the flowers unfold, new-born lambs prance in the fields. Then the corn ripens, and the apples start to go red on the trees. The air is still, and noisy with humming insects. But once high summer is past, autumn draws near, and soon Persephone must go back to her underground kingdom. When she goes, the leaves fall from the trees, mist creeps up from the river valleys and low clouds rest on the mountains. The plants shrivel with cold, and men hunch their shoulders as they walk. Winter has come to the earth, to grip it cruelly, until Persephone comes again in the spring.

The Fugitive

The Fugitive

The story of one of the defeated at Troy

"I AM a refugee. It distresses me to tell my story, for it revives the memory of much unhappiness—but here it is.

"The Greeks had been beseiging Troy for many years, and had achieved nothing. Then they built an enormous horse, with sides made of planks of wood. They left it outside the walls of the city, and then set sail. They hid themselves on an island a little offshore, but we Trojans all thought they had gone home to Mycenae. We rushed out of the gates of Troy and rejoiced to see the Greek camp deserted at last. Above all, we marvelled at the huge wooden horse. Soon there were fierce arguments between those who wanted to bring it

inside our city walls, and those who wanted to hurl it into the sea.

"Laocoon, a priest, came running to join in the argument.

" 'This is some plot of the Greeks. Surely you know by now how wily Odysseus is, and how many schemes spring from his cunning brain? I fear the Greeks, even when they seem to come bearing gifts.'

"He hurled his spear at the side of the wooden horse. If only we had all joined him and destroyed the creature, the lofty towers of Troy would be standing now. But just then a Greek captive was brought before us.

"' Everyone is against me!' he exclaimed in despair. 'The Greeks have been plotting to take my life because wily Odysseus hates me, and now I am your prisoner.'

"Out of pity, we took the chains off his wrist.

" 'What is this wooden horse for?' we asked him eagerly.

" 'It is an offering to the goddess Athene. So long as it remains outside your walls, the Greeks will conquer Troy, but if you once drag it inside you will be victorious and carry the war from Troy to all the cities of Greece itself.'

"From the moment he spoke these lies, the downfall of Troy began. The first to suffer was Laocoon, the priest who urged us to have nothing to do with the horse. Two enormous snakes came out of the sea, and started to writhe their way over the foreshore. Their tongues darted in and out of their mouths. They made straight for where Laocoon was doing sacrifice at an altar, and coiled themselves round his two young sons who were standing beside him. He tried to hack them off, but they wrapped themselves round him as well, tighter and tighter, crushing the life out of him.

"We remembered how he had hurled his spear at the horse, and thought that this must be a punishment for his impiety. We put rollers under the horse's feet and thick ropes round its neck, and hastened to drag it into our city. It was too big to go through the gates, so we broke down a part of the city walls. So we dragged it in, with boys and unmarried girls singing joyfully around it. Four times it got stuck, but we dragged harder then ever, until we had pulled it inside. Then, in our crazy folly, we went to put flowers on all the shrines in the city.

"Night came, and we went to sleep. The Greek army came out of their hiding place on the island, and sailed again towards Troy. Meanwhile Sinon, the Greek captive, who had lied to us about the horse, crept out into the streets. He unlocked a little door under the horse's belly, and some Greek soldiers slid down a rope to the ground. One of them was Odysseus, the most cunning of men. They killed all our sentries and flung open our gates for their main army to come in.

"I was slow to wake up, for the house where my father, Anchises, lived lay set back from the street and was sheltered by trees. As I dragged myself from sleep, I could hear the clatter of fighting and the soughing noise of flames. I seized my arms and dashed into the street. The city was in confusion. Fire roared, leaping from house to house, the Greeks rushed through the streets, killing whoever stood in their way. The tall towers on the battlements came crashing down. We seized on the debris and anything else we could use for missiles against the unending hail of arrows and spears. Women shrieked with terror, and still the Greek soldiers surged in, like a river bursting its banks.

"Priam, our aged king, put on the armour he had worn in his youth. He hurled his spear at one of the Greeks, but he no longer had any strength. The spear struck harmlessly on a shield, and the Greek killed him.

"Suddenly, I realized that I alone was left, of all the

Trojan warriors. I hesitated, not knowing what to do, when my mother who was a goddess, suddenly appeared before me, beautiful and radiant as she appears in heaven.

" 'You must flee, my son, and I will watch over you. But first go and see if your family are alive.'

"With these words, she vanished. I hurried back to my father's house.

" 'We must hurry away,' I said.

" 'I mean to die here,' objected my father.

"My wife, Creusa, and our son, Ascanius, begged him to come, but he would not move until suddenly a tongue of flame started to flicker on Ascanius's head. It caressed his hair, but did not burn it. In great alarm, Creusa and I hurried to put out the fire, but my father lifted his hands in prayer.

" 'Confirm this omen,' he begged.

"A shooting star fell to earth with a trail of brilliant fire.

" 'I will come,' said my father.

"So we set off through the burning city. I carried my old father on my shoulders and held Ascanius by the band. He had to hurry to keep up with my longer strides. My wife followed some way behind with our servants, so that we would not call attention to ourselves by being too large a group.

" 'If you lose sight of us, we will wait for you at the deserted temple by a cypress tree,' I told her.

"We made our way through the streets, keeping in the shadows by the sides of the houses. I trembled at every breeze. Suddenly, we heard footsteps.

" 'Run!' urged my father.

"I hurried off through a maze of alleys, until at last we got safely outside the walls and found the deserted temple. I waited until all the others came up, but my wife was not there. What could have happened to her? Had she lost her way, or had she been overcome by exhaustion?

"Once again, I risked my life by going back into the city. It was uncannily quiet now, and all the lights were quenched. I went back to our own house, but she was not there. I stumbled on through the streets. Once I saw wily Odysseus and another Greek keeping guard over all the treasure they had looted from us. Once I saw a huddle of frightened mothers and children. I became so rash that I called aloud, 'Creusa!' again and again.

"Suddenly she appeared, or rather her ghostly shape, larger than life. My hair stood on end, and I could not speak.

" 'The gods did not want me to come with you,' she said gently. 'You are going to travel a very long way, until you get to Italy, where your destiny lies. Look after our son.'

"I tried to fling my arms round her neck, but three times she slipped away from me, like the wind. At last I gave up, and went back to my father. Many others had joined our group. They were anxious to be our companions in exile.

"Morning came. A great force of Greeks held the city. I picked up my father again, and led the way to the mountains."

This is the story which Aeneas, a prince of Troy, told to Dido, the Queen of Carthage. He had reached Carthage after many adventures. Dido, who loved him, wished him to stay there, but as the ghost of Creusa had said, his destiny was to go on to Italy. There he founded a city. Many years later, his descendants founded another, the greatest city that there has ever been in the world. It was called Rome.

The Uninvited Guests

The story of one of the victors at Troy

The Uninvited Guests

The story of one of the victors at Troy

THE seige of Troy had dragged on for ten years, and now it was nearly ten years since the siege was over. All the Greek kings and princes who had fought and conquered at Troy had reached home many years before, all except one. That was Odysseus, king of the island of Ithaca, who was the wisest and subtlest of all the Greeks.

Odysseus had sailed from Troy nearly ten years before, thinking that he would have a quick passage home. On his way, he met many strange adventures.

He went to the island of the Cyclops, a terrible one-eyed giant. The Cyclops imprisoned Odysseus and his men in a cave. Odysseus blinded the Cyclops and got his men away by a trick. This proved to be the source of a great deal of trouble. For the Cyclops was the son of the sea god, who vowed, in revenge, that Odysseus would not reach Ithaca for many long years, and that when he did, he would find trouble in his own home.

So, more terrible adventures beset him. He sailed to the island of Circe, a powerful enchantress, and she turned his men into pigs. Odysseus persuaded her to restore them all to their proper shape, but it was a full year before he got away from the island. Even then, he did not know how he would reach home safely. He went down into the underworld, where the souls of the dead live, to consult a dead prophet there. Hardly any man had made this journey and come back alive. He spoke to the prophet, who replied to him gravely.

"The sea god is still very angry with you. You may reach home safely with all your men, but it will be very difficult.

Whatever you do, you must not kill the cattle which belong to the sun god."

Odysseus came back to earth, and his troubles started again. He sailed past the island of the sirens, creatures who sang so beautifully that all the passing ships landed to hear them better. Then the sirens would tear the sailors to pieces and eat their flesh. Luckily, Odysseus knew what to do, for Circe had warned him. He put melted wax in the ears of his men, so that they could not hear the song, and got them to lash him to the mast. The men rowed past the island, while Odysseus, ravished by the song, struggled to break free.

After that, they had to sail through a narrow stretch of water between two dreadful rocks. On one side, lived a creature called Scylla, who snatched sailors out of every ship that went past. On the other side, was a violent whirlpool called Charybdis, in which many ships had been wrecked. They managed to keep away from Charybdis, but only by sailing close to Scylla, who snatched six of their men.

The worst was still to come. They landed on the island where the sun god kept his cattle. In spite of the warning that Odysseus gave them, his men killed some of the cattle, because they were feeling so hungry. They set sail again, but, in his anger, the sun god had their ship wrecked. Only Odysseus was left. He lashed two pieces of timber together, and for nine days he drifted on them. On the tenth day, he was thrown up on the island where the nymph Calypso lived. But the sea god had not forgiven him yet for having blinded the Cyclops. He made Calypso fall in love with Odysseus, and she kept him, on her island, for seven years. Nobody, in the world outside, knew what had happened to him. Gradually everyone came to think that he must be dead.

When Odysseus had sailed for Troy, so many years before, he had left behind his wife called Penelope, and a baby son called Telemachus. Penelope was very beautiful. She was also very sweet-tempered and well-mannered, and ran her household skilfully. In fact, she was an ideal wife. Unfortunately, this occurred to a great many people. All the kings and princes of the islands round Ithaca started to say to themselves, "Odysseus will never come back. Penelope is bound to get married again. She is much too beautiful not to. Why shouldn't she marry me?" So all the local princes went to Ithaca to woo Penelope, taking their servants with them. Penelope received them politely, because she had no idea what she was letting herself in for. For the princes all settled down in the palace at Ithaca, and vowed that they would not go home until she had made up her mind which one she was going to marry. They had a wonderful time, feasting on all Odysseus's sheep and pigs, and gulping his wine. When they were not feasting, they lounged around playing draughts, or making advances to Penelope's maids. Their servants were a nuisance as well. They were far too grand, with their scented, curled hair, to help with any hard work.

Poor Penelope did not know what to do. She hated having these uninvited guests in her house, but the only way to get rid of them was to marry again. She hated the idea of this even more. No other man, certainly none of her greedy suitors, could ever compare to Odysseus. She hit on a cunning scheme. She said she could never marry before she had woven a shroud for Odysseus's old father, who was so upset by the loss of his son that he might not live much longer. For three years she wove it, but every night, by torchlight, she used to undo what she did in the daytime. Then her maids betrayed the trick. The angry suitors compelled her to finish the shroud. Now, she could not think how to defer her marriage. To make things worse, her parents were urging her to get married again. They said that she had spent long enough crying over Odysseus. Even her son, Telemachus, wanted her to get married. He was now grown up, and he longed to manage his own lands in peace. not have a crowd of wastrels eating up all his livestock and drinking all his wine.

Luckily for Odysseus, the goddess Athene felt very sorry for him. When the sea god went off on a visit to the Ethiopians, she took advantage of his absence to persuade all the other gods to let Odysseus come home.

"I shall go to Ithaca myself and stir Telemachus up," she said. "The son of a brave man like Odysseus ought to show a little more spirit. All he does, is to dream about his father's return. It's time he did something about that crowd of gluttons and drunkards himself."

She disguised herself as a chieftain, and went to Ithaca. Odysseus's house was full of his uninvited guests. They were all swaggering round as if they owned the place. She talked to Telemachus, and said how dreadfully the suitors were all behaving. He did not know who she was, but when she left, he had a strange feeling that he had been visited by an immortal. He felt inspired to speak to his guests severely.

"I can't carry on like this, with you eating me out of house and home. I am going to seek news of my father, from the men who fought with him at Troy. If I hear he is still alive, I will let you stay for another year, while he is getting home. If he is dead, I will put up a monument to him, and give my mother's hand in marriage to a new husband. Then the rest of you can get out."

So Telemachus set off, with Athene's help. She thought that the trip would be good for him, and give him the self-command that Odysseus's son should possess.

In the meantime, the gods sent a messenger to Calypso, to persuade her to let Odysseus go. She agreed reluctantly. She helped Odysseus to build a boat, and he set sail again. For seventeen days, all went well. Then the sea god came back from his visit to the Ethiopians. He was furious to discover that Odysseus had escaped. He sent a terrible storm, and wrecked Odysseus's ship. Odysseus was thrown into the surging water, with only a beam to cling to. He struggled towards the shore. The surf was so fierce that he might never have landed, if Athene had not directed him to a sheltered place near the mouth of a stream. There he was found by the daughter of the king of that country. She took him home to her parents, who welcomed him and entertained him. In the end, they provided a ship to take him home to Ithaca. He was fast asleep when they reached the island, so the sailors picked him up and laid him carefully on the sand, and left him there. Even so, the sea god had not exhausted his malice, for he turned the ship into a rock on her homeward voyage.

When Odysseus woke up, it was very misty. It was such a long time since he had been home that he could not recognize where he was. He felt bitterly disappointed, and thought that the sailors had tricked him. Just then, Athene appeared, disguised as a young shepherd. She wanted to stop him going straight to his house, in case Penelope's jealous suitors should band together and kill him.

"Where am I?" Odysseus asked wretchedly.

"In Ithaca," answered Athene.

Now Odysseus had always been very cautious and cunning. He did not know what had been happening during his long absence, and he did not wish to reveal who he was until he knew more about things. He pretended that he was a fugitive running away from Crete. Athene, of course, saw through his pretence. She turned herself into her own likeness of a beautiful woman.

"How typical of you, Odysseus, not to rush at things. You are going to need all your cunning. Your court has been taken over by a gang of uninvited guests. They are eating your food, doing what they like with your servants, and, worst of all, they are trying to marry your wife. She has managed to play them off, one against the other, but, even so, things are terribly difficult for her. Let's make a plan. I will disguise you as an old beggar for the time being, so that no one will recognize you, not even your wife. Then you must approach the swineherd who is in charge of the pigs. He has always been loyal to your interests, and he will help us. I will go to bring back Telemachus, who has gone to get news of you from some of your old companions."

"Why didn't you tell him that I was alive? You knew that I was," said Odysseus.

"The journey will add to his reputation, and will help make a man of him," answered Athene.

With that, she touched Odysseus with her wand. His hair fell out, his skin shrivelled up, and his clothes turned into filthy rags. He made his way towards the head swineherd's farm. As he approached, the dogs flew at him, because he looked like a beggar. They would have savaged him, if the swineherd had not thrown a stone and sent them away.

"That was a narrow escape!" said the swineherd. "We don't want any more disasters. It's bad enough having my master away, and no one knows if he'll come back. Then there's that horde of thieves, for that's all they are, who have taken over his house. They slaughter the pigs as fast as I get them fattened, and they drink themselves silly. Come and have something to eat."

He prepared them both a meal in his house, and then started talking again.

"These are only little pigs that I'm giving you. All the best beasts go to that rabble who are wooing my master's wife."

It was obvious to Odysseus that the swineherd was still

loyal to him. It was also obvious that he had been doing his job very faithfully. He had looked after the herds of swine, and had built them some fine new sties in the farmyard. Odysseus wondered how he could use the swineherd to help him, and started to question him, cautiously and obliquely.

"What is your master's name? Maybe I've come across him somewhere. I've been all over the place."

"My master's name was Odysseus. There's plenty of charlatans come to the palace who pretend to have met him. It's an easy way of getting a night's lodging. No, I'm afraid that he's dead. What worries me now is young Telemachus. He went off to look for his father, and now that gang who've invited themselves to his house are planning to kill him on his way back. But tell me about yourself."

In answer, Odysseus told him a very long story, which was completely untrue. He still had not decided how to tackle the problems that faced him. The swineherd believed every word, except when he pretended to have met Odysseus on his wanderings. Then they had another meal, this time of one of the best fatted pigs that were normally kept for the suitors. Odysseus lay down to sleep afterwards, but the loyal swineherd went out to keep watch over the pigs.

In the meantime, Athene went to Telemachus, and told him to come home. She warned him to be very careful, and not to travel by the obvious route, as his mother's suitors were plotting to ambush him. If he landed safely in Ithaca, he was to go to the swineherd's house, to find out what the situation was.

In due course, Telemachus reached the island, and did as Athene had told him. The swineherd was delighted to see him again. Odysseus, who was there, pretended not to recognize him, while Telemachus had no idea that the old beggar was really his father. But Athene, who had been watching, thought it was time for the two of them to get together. She touched Odysseus with her wand, and made him look once again like a man in the prime of life. At first, Telemachus thought that he must be a god, to have changed so miraculously. When at last he was persuaded that his father had really come home again after so many years, he was overwhelmed with emotion.

"We must plan what to do to get rid of our uninvited guests," said Odysseus.

"You don't know what you're saying, Father. Why, there must be a hundred of them, not to mention their servants."

"Yes, but I have a plan, and the gods will help us. You go back home, and don't tell your mother about this. I'll follow you, disguised as a beggar again. You mustn't appear to know me, whatever happens, until I give you a nod. Then, make some excuse to get all available weapons out of the way, just leaving enough for us."

The suitors were very surprised when they heard that Telemachus had escaped the ambush. They pretended to welcome him home, but in fact they were wondering what further harm they could do him. They still showed no signs of trying to leave the palace, but went on with their old ways. They amused themselves with quoits and with throwing the javelin, and ordered an enormous meal of sheep and goats, pigs and a young calf.

Later that day, Odysseus went back to his own house. The swineherd came with him to show him the way, although really he knew it perfectly well already. As they approached the palace, they could smell all the meat roasting for the feast. By the gate, they saw an old dog covered with fleas. Many years ago, before Odysseus had sailed for Troy, he had trained this dog, which was called Argus. When Argus saw Odysseus, he knew at once who it was. He wagged his tail, and lay back his ears. He had not got enough strength to get up and come nearer. Then he died, happy that his master had come home at last.

Odysseus was secretly very moved, but he was still acting the part of an old beggar. He went into the great hall and started to ask for food. Most of the suitors gave him something, but one threw a stool at his shoulder. He went out, and got into a fight with another beggar, and beat him soundly. This entertained the suitors, who were always looking for distraction, and they let him come back into the hall. There he saw Penelope, for the first time since his return. She was looking extremely beautiful. It was obvious that all the suitors admired her, and equally obvious that she did not want to have anything to do with any of them. He stayed in the hall, after they all went to bed.

"Telemachus," he said, "hide all the weapons now."

Telemachus went off to do so, and Penelope came into the hall to question her guest.

"You can see what position I'm in," she said. "These uninvited guests are beggaring me. My parents are urging me to get married again, and I know that my son wants me to, before all his patrimony is destroyed. But now, tell me who you are."

Once again, Odysseus repeated his lying story, pretending that he was a Cretan. "And I met Odysseus once," he ended. "He stayed with me for twelve days."

Penelope started to cry for her lost husband, who was, in fact, sitting beside her. Even then, Odysseus did not relent and say who he was, in case this spoilt all his plans.

"What was he wearing?" Penelope asked. She thought that this might help to show her if the story was true.

"He was wearing a fine purple cloak, and a brooch made of gold with a hound and a deer on it."

Penelope started to cry again, for she recognized the things from his description.

"Don't cry. From all I hear, Odysseus will be back in a year," he said.

"I only hope that you're right. In the meantime, you must stay in our house for a while. I'll send one of my maids to wash your feet."

"I don't want girls messing around with my feet, not at my time of life. I'd rather have a woman of my own age."

"Then my husband's old nurse can do it," Penelope answered.

The nurse fetched a basin of water. Suddenly, it struck Odysseus that she might recognize an old scar on his thigh, where a wild boar had wounded him, many years before. He turned away from the firelight, but he was too late. The old nurse saw the scar, and dropped the basin of water. It spilt all over the floor, but she took no notice of it.

"Odysseus!" she exclaimed.

"Quiet! If you tell anyone, I'll kill you."

"Don't talk to me like that, my boy," answered his nurse. "You know I can hold my tongue."

She went off to fetch another basin of water. When she had finished washing his feet, Penelope spoke once again.

"If I have to marry again, I shall test my suitors. My husband Odysseus used to set up twelve axes in a row, and shoot them all down. I shall make my suitors try to do this, and marry the most skilful."

This served Odysseus's purpose extremely well.

"Yes, do this," he said.

Then Penelope went to bed. As soon as she was alone in her room, she broke down and wept yet once more for her lost husband.

Next day, the servants made the palace ready for still more

feasting. Odysseus, in his disguise as a beggar, watched them. He got talking to the chief cow-man, who had just driven a heifer and some goats in for the feast.

"If only Odysseus would come back—and I haven't given up hope—he'd find out how loyal I have been to him, all this long time," said the cow-man.

Then the uninvited guests trooped in to dine. Before that, they had been busy plotting how they could kill Telemachus. They fell greedily to their food. One of them picked up a cow's hoof, and threw it at the old beggar. Odysseus ducked, and it hit the wall instead. They all joked and shouted. At one moment, they were helpless with laughter. Next moment, they were crying sentimentally, without even knowing what they were crying about. They became more and more drunk. All this time, Telemachus kept an eye on Odysseus, to wait for his signal. Before anything could happen, Penelope decided to test her suitors. She carried Odysseus's great bow into the hall, and her women followed, carrying twelve axes.

"I am challenging you to a trial of skill," she said. "I have decided to marry whatever man is most skilful at stringing this bow and at shooting an arrow through these twelve axes."

The swineherd and the cow-man were full of sorrow to think that she should marry again. Telemachus set the axes into the ground. Then, one by one, the suitors tried to string Odysseus's bow. It was so big and heavy that they could not even bend the bow to string it. They tried greasing it with hot tallow to make the bow more supple, but still they did not succeed.

Meanwhile, Odysseus went out into the courtyard with the swineherd and the head cow-man. At last the time had come to reveal who he was. When they heard that their master had come home, after so many years, they were overjoyed.

Odysseus gave them some instructions about what to do. Then they went back into the hall.

"Will you let me try my hand at the bow?" he asked.

"You're drunk, you old beggar, to suggest it," the suitors shouted.

While they were shouting and arguing, the swineherd picked up the bow and gave it to Odysseus. Then he told his old nurse to see that all the women were safely locked up in their own part of the house, well out of the way of what was going to happen. The cow-man barred the door so that nobody could get out, and Odysseus stationed himself beside it. He felt the bow to make sure that the wood was not worm-eaten after all these years. Then, without any fuss or difficulty, he bent the great bow and strung it. He twanged on the string. Then he picked up an arrow and shot it, straight through the twelve axes. After this, he gave a nod to Telemachus.

This was the signal, and with that, he shot dead one of the uninvited guests who were plundering his own house. For a moment, the others thought that this was an accident, but Odysseus soon disillusioned them.

"You never thought to see me alive," he shouted. "You have been eating me out of house and home, and wooing my own wife. Don't expect any mercy."

"We'll pay you back for what we have eaten," shouted one of the suitors.

"You must pay for your crimes as well," Odysseus retorted grimly.

At that, one of them rushed forward with his sword, but Odysseus shot him dead. Telemachus went to fetch more weapons. The suitors were at a disadvantage, because all their own weapons had been hidden away. Odysseus went on shooting them, one by one, until he had used all his arrows. Then he had a set-back. A servant, who was loyal to the suitors, managed to creep out of the hall by a side-door. He made his way to the armoury, where Telemachus had foolishly left the door open. He managed to smuggle a pile of swords and shields in to the suitors. Now the fight became desperate. The suitors hurled their lances in a frantic effort to kill Odysseus, but Athene was determined not to let them succeed. Suddenly, Odysseus and his supporters charged through the hall, hacking right and left with their swords. They did not stop until, with the help of Athene, they had killed all the rest of the suitors.

They started to clear up the hall, and the nurse came out to help.

"Fetch me Penelope," Odysseus commanded.

"Put some decent clothes on," said the old woman.

"We'll get the house properly clean first," Odysseus retorted. He went round the house, fumigating it with hot sulphur. While he was doing this, the nurse hurried off to Penelope's room, chuckling with delight.

"Odysseus has come home, my dear. He was disguised as a beggar. And now he's got rid of those creatures who have been pestering us for so long. He's killed the whole pack of them."

Penelope was as cautious as her husband.

"I can't really believe you, but I'll come down and see just what's happened."

She went into the hall, and sat down opposite Odysseus. She stared at him, but would not say anything until she was sure who he was. She was frightened he might be somebody tricking her.

"That's not much of a welcome for my father," Telemachus remonstrated.

"If it's really Odysseus, I will find out," said Penelope.

Odysseus went off to have a bath, and to put proper

clothes on, instead of his rags. When he came back, Penelope still would not speak.

"What a wife!" he exclaimed. "Any other woman would be delighted to have me back, after nineteen years."

"I've got to be sure," said Penelope. "Nurse, make him up a bed for the night. Take the big bed out of Odysseus's old bedroom."

She said this as a test, to find out who he really was.

"How can you do that?" Odysseus demanded. "The bed-post is a tree trunk that's rooted into the ground. I know, for I made it myself."

With that, Penelope knew that her husband had really come back.

Next day, Odysseus went to see his old father. He had suffered dreadfully during Odysseus's absence. His wife had died of grief, because she believed that their son was dead. Now the old man was working and living like a farm labourer, because he was too wretched to care about anything. He wore filthy old clothes, and would not even bother to sleep in a proper bed. When Odysseus found him, he was hoeing in a vineyard. Odysseus wanted to know how his father felt after all these years.

"Is this really Ithaca?" he demanded. "I met a man from Ithaca called Odysseus, about four years ago. I hoped he'd be back here by now."

His father was overcome by grief, thinking this proved that Odysseus must be dead. Odysseus regretted his caution.

"I am your son," he cried. "I've come home and killed that gang who were ruining me."

His father was cautious in his turn.

"What proof can you give me?"

"I can show you the scar where I was wounded by a boar's tusk. Or I can tell you about the trees on this terrace. When I was a little boy, you gave me thirteen pear-trees, ten apple-trees, and forty fig-trees, as well as fifty rows of vines."

His father now knew who he was. So Odysseus was reunited with all his own family. He lived until he was old, and ruled Ithaca in peace, now that he had rid his house of his uninvited guests.

Swimming to School

Swimming to School

A BOY who lived on the shores of the Bay of Naples used to go to school in a town four miles from his home. There were a lot of dolphins which lived in the bay, and the boy became very fond of one of them. Although they live in the water, dolphins are animals, not fish. He used to go to the water's edge and call for this dolphin. When it came, he gave it scraps of bread. It grew to know his voice, and would come whenever he called. Then, one day, it became even more friendly. It lowered the sharp fins on its back, so that they would not prick anybody, and rolled about in the water, gazing up at the boy. At last he guessed what it meant. He climbed on the dolphin's back, and away they went together, plunging up and down in the warm, blue sea.

They both enjoyed it so much that the dolphin started to take him to school every day. It swam all the way from Baiae, where the boy lived, to another town on the coast, called Puteoli, where he went to school. Then, when the boy's lessons were over, it would swim him back home again. How the other boys envied him! No one had ever ridden to school on a dolphin before, and no one has done so since.

How Thor Fooled the Giants

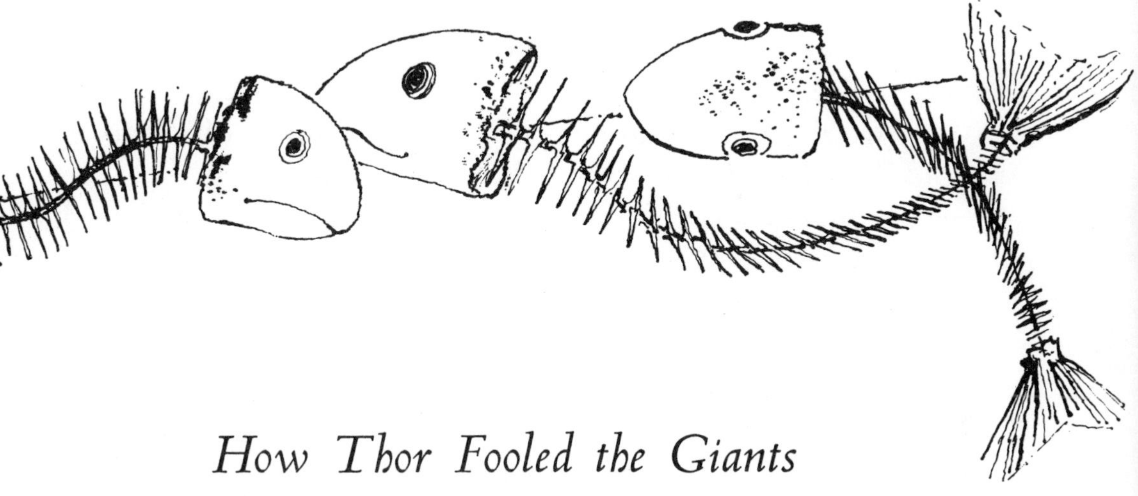

How Thor Fooled the Giants

THOR was the god of Thunder, a strong, tough man with a bristling red beard that shook violently when he was angry. It shook very fiercely one morning when he woke up and found that someone had stolen his miraculous hammer.

"How can I make the thunder now my hammer's been stolen?" he shouted.

Thor's voice was very loud indeed, even when he was talking normally. The other gods used to keep a little away from him, because it hurt if he talked too close to their ears. When he was angry, his voice sounded as loud as the thunder itself, when it echoes round the snow-covered mountains.

"What shall I do?" bellowed Thor.

"Come and ask Freya," said Loki, the god of Fire. He was usually the most unkind of gods, but today he was feeling helpful. They hurried to Asgarth, the home of the gods, where Freya, the beautiful goddess of Spring, was sitting. She had golden hair, the colour of the wild daffodils that come when the snow has gone, and her eyes were as blue as the sky on the first sunny day of spring.

"Lend us your magic coat of feathers," demanded Thor. He was one of those people who think it a waste of time to be very polite.

"I would lend it to you even if it was made of silver or gold," said Freya. She wanted a quiet time, alone with her own thoughts, and this seemed as good a way as any of getting rid of that noisy Thor.

In the end, though, it was Loki who put on the magic cloak of feathers. Thor was too big for it. So Loki flew off, with the feathers rustling, to Jotunheim, the land of the giants. This was a land of huge mountains that were always covered with snow. The only rivers were rivers of ice. There, on a desolate, icy mountain, he found Thrym, the lord of the giants. He was smoothing the manes of his horses, and was twisting long strips of gold into collars for his greyhounds.

"How are things going in the land of the gods?" he greeted Loki. "And why have you come to Jotunheim all by yourself?"

"Things are going badly," Loki replied. "Have you stolen Thor's hammer that he uses to make the thunder?"

Thrym parted his lips a little, and grinned. His beard was so matted with frost that it looked like long icicles hanging down from his chin.

"I have hidden Thor's hammer eight miles under the earth. No one shall get it back, until they bring me the beautiful goddess Freya to be my bride."

Without saying another word, Loki flew back to the land of the gods. The first person he saw was Thor.

"What luck?" Thor demanded.

"Everything's all right. He'll give it back, but he says he

must marry Freya first. I suppose that we'd better go and tell her.''

They hurried off to find her.

''Come on, Freya,'' said Thor, as soon as he saw her. ''Put on a white dress or something. You're going to marry Thrym.''

Freya breathed very deeply. Her golden hair crackled with anger. Her blue eyes were as chilly as the blue ice of a glacier.

''Me marry Thrym? Me marry one of those giants? What do you take me for?''

All the gods hurried together to see what the matter was. One of them had an idea.

''Why don't we dress up Thor like a bride? We could cover his head up. Then he could go to Jotunheim and try to get back his hammer.''

''You won't get me pretending to be a woman,'' growled Thor. ''I'd never live it down.''

''Stop being so silly,'' said Loki severely. ''Unless we get your hammer back, the giants will be stronger than us. They might even invade our country. After all, it's a much better place to live than where they do.''

With a very bad grace indeed, Thor let himself be dressed up as a bride. They hung precious jewels round his neck, and swathed his head with fine white veiling. They took special care to cover his eyes, which were bloodshot and very angry.

''You look just like a bride,'' said Freya, trying to cheer him up.

''Grrrrrr,'' growled Thor, who was too cross even to talk.

Loki was dressed up as a serving maid, and together they travelled to the land of the giants. With great ceremony, they were shown into caverns, eight miles under the ground. They went into a huge hall that was splendid with a red and white stalactite ceiling. Huge tables were laid ready for a feast.

"Welcome," said Thrym. "Welcome to the land of the giants. I have cattle with golden horns, and the finest black oxen you ever saw, and many other treasures as well. Now I have the only thing that was lacking, the beautiful Freya to be my bride."

They started the feast. The great ceremonial cup of ale was borne round the hall. Thor was given some dainty food, suitable for a bride. He started to feel very hungry. Titbits were no good to him. There were three whole salmon in front of him, so he ate them to be going on with. Then he ate an ox roasted whole, that was meant to serve everyone at the table. He still had a few odd spaces to fill, so he ate another five salmon. All this gave him a bit of a thirst, so he drank three full cups of mead, which was all he could lay hands on for the moment.

"Did you ever see a girl with an appetite like that?" Thrym exclaimed. He sounded very proud, but also a little bit doubtful. He was probably wondering how much it would cost to feed her.

Loki was very afraid that Thrym would guess what was happening. He tried to think of a convincing story.

"Freya hasn't been able to eat for over a week," he whispered. "She was so anxious to see you."

Thrym was delighted to hear this. He stooped down and lifted the veil from his bride's face so he could kiss her. Then he gave a jump. He jumped right to the back of his enormous hall.

"Whatever is wrong with Freya's eyes?" he gasped. "They look as if they're on fire."

"It's all right," said Loki soothingly. "She hasn't slept for over a week because she's been thinking of you all the time."

"Bring me Thor's magic hammer," Thrym shouted. "I want to lay it on the lap of my bride as a wedding token."

The hammer was brought, and Thor gave a loud bellow of joy. He flung back his veil and seized it from Thrym's hand. He waved it above his head. Then, single-handed, he knocked out all the giants in the hall. He flung his veil to the ground and trampled on it, he pulled off his silly long skirts and trampled on them as well.

"That'll show 'em," growled Thor.

So that was how Thor got back his hammer.

How the Giants Fooled Thor

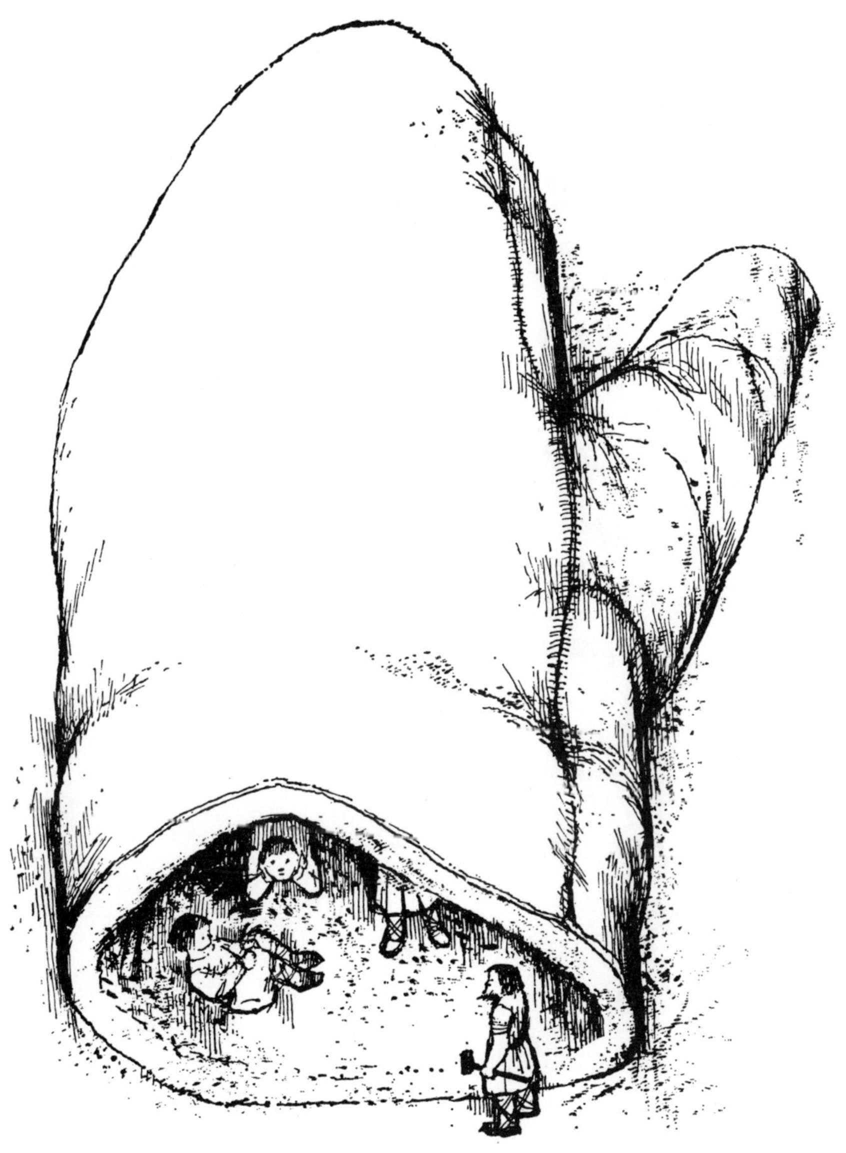

How the Giants Fooled Thor

THOR and Loki and two companions went on an expedition to the land of the giants. They walked all day through a wood, and when it was dark, they found an enormous hall. They went in through the door, which was the width of one whole side, and settled down for the night. At midnight, they were woken up by an earthquake, and took shelter in a side-room. Outside, they heard a terrible muffled roar.

Next morning, Thor went out, gripping his hammer tightly. He saw a giant fast asleep. It was his snores they had heard. Suddenly, the giant woke up.

"What's your name?" Thor demanded.

"Skrymir, that means Big Fellow," the giant replied. "And you're Thor, aren't you? Where's my glove got to?" He picked up the glove, and Thor realized that this was the "hall" where they had spent the night. The "side-room" had been the thumb.

"Let's travel together," Skrymir suggested. They all sat down to breakfast. When they had finished, he said, "Suppose we pool our provisions. Give me your food, and I'll carry the whole lot."

He strode off, with the food in a bag on his shoulder, and they hurried along behind him. When the evening came, he settled down under an oak tree.

"I'm going to sleep, so get your own supper, Thor."

In a moment, he was asleep.

Thor was very hungry by now. He tried to undo the bag, but the knots were too tight. He got crosser and crosser, and all the while he struggled he felt more and more hungry. In the end, he was so annoyed, that he picked up his hammer, and hit Skrymir on the head.

"Eh? What was that?" muttered Skrymir. "Oh, a leaf fell down from the tree. I expect you've finished your supper now. Hope you've enjoyed it. Goodnight."

He dropped off to sleep again. Thor waited until he was snoring, and then hit him even harder. The top of his hammer sunk into Skrymir's face.

"Oh, drat this tree. An acorn fell on my face. What, are you still about, Thor?"

"I'm just going to bed."

Thor sat and waited. Next time, he told himself, he would finish the giant off. At last, he heard Skrymir snoring again. He lifted his hammer, and hit him the hardest blow he had ever dealt in his life. The hammer sank in right up to the handle.

"Something fell on my cheek," grumbled Skrymir. "Are there any birds in that tree? Messy creatures, aren't they? Why don't you get your clothes on, Thor? I'm off in a moment. If you travel on in the direction you're going, you'll get to Utgard. You'll see some really fine men there, much bigger then me. Or perhaps, if you've got any sense, you'll go back to where you came from."

He strode off, taking their food in his bag with him.

"Hope I never see him again!" Thor exclaimed. "Let's go and have a look at this place."

They walked on until they came to a stronghold. It was so big that they had to tilt their heads right back to see over the top. No one came to let them in, but at last they managed to squeeze through the bars of the gate. They went into a hall where some giants were sitting. They greeted the one who looked like the king, but for a long time he took no notice of them at all. At last he said, "What? Is this guttersnipe really Thor? I thought Thor was supposed to be strong. What do you all imagine that you are good at? I won't have you here unless you can prove you are really skilful at something."

"I am skilful," said Loki. "I can eat faster than anyone else."

"Let's test you, then," said the Giant King.

He called for a huge platter of meat, and Loki and one of the giants began to gobble away together. Soon Loki had eaten everything but the bones, but the giant had eaten the bones and the plate as well.

"And how about that youngster there?" asked the Giant King. He pointed at young Thjalfi, who was one of Thor's companions.

"I can run faster than anyone else," said Thjalfi.

"Let's try you then," said the Giant King. He beckoned to one of his men.

They ran three races altogether. Each time, the giant ran so fast that he had turned back to meet Thjalfi before Thjalfi had got half-way.

"Not much doubt about who won that," said the Giant King. "Now, Thor, how about you?"

"I'll show my skill at drinking."

The Giant King called for a horn.

"It's good going if you can empty this horn in one go.

Some men take two, but no one is such a poor drinker that he can't down the lot in three."

Thor took the horn. It was not very big, although it was rather long. He gulped and gulped, and at last stopped to draw breath. He looked into the horn and saw that the liquid had hardly gone down at all.

"I'd have never believed it if someone had told me that that was all Thor could drink!" said the Giant King in amazement. "Still, I know you'll empty it next time."

Thor tried again. He drank until he was out of breath, but still the drink had hardly gone down any more.

"You've left a lot for your last attempt," said the Giant King.

Thor drank furiously. He tried to tilt the horn right up, but he could not, he drank and drank until he was nearly bursting. At last he stopped. There was a slight difference but that was all.

"Perhaps you're better at something else," suggested the Giant King. "Suppose you try picking my cat up? We think of that as a children's game, and I wouldn't like to suggest it, except I see Thor is not nearly as strong as he is cracked up to be."

A grey cat jumped on to the floor. It was a giant cat, to match the rest of the place. Thor put his hands under its belly, and pushed and heaved. The cat's back arched. At last Thor pushed hard enough to lift one of its paws off the ground, but that was all he could do.

"It's a big cat, of course," said the Giant King. "And Thor's only a little fellow."

"You can call me little, if you like, but I'll show you. You're making me really cross. Somebody come and wrestle with me!"

"But there's nobody feeble enough for you. Oh, I know. We'll send for an old woman."

The old woman came, and they wrestled. Quite soon, she had forced Thor down on to one knee.

Next morning, they left. The Giant King came with them out of the stronghold, to say goodbye.

"What did you think of us all?" he asked.

"I don't mind admitting that you've humiliated me," said Thor, in a rueful voice.

"Now we're out of my stronghold, I'll tell you the truth—and I'll never let you into my stronghold again. I am really the giant you met in the wood. I tied up the bag of provisions with iron wires, that's why you couldn't undo it. Then I deceived you with magic spells. When you thought you were hitting my head, you were hitting those mountains there. The valleys are the dents that your hammers left. If you had really hit me, you'd have killed me with the first blow, and that was the gentlest of all. Then, as to those contests. First of all Loki was eating fast, but his opponent was really Fire, that swallows everything up. Next, when Thjalfi was running, he was running against Thought, which is quicker than anybody. And then, when you were drinking, and I'd never have thought you could have done it, the other end of the drinking horn was in the sea. Just look at the sea, and you'll find how much you have drained it. As for the cat, you terrified us when you managed to shift its paw. It was really the great serpent, which is curled round the earth. And it was wonderful, how well you held out in the wrestling match. You were fighting against an enemy that no one can overcome, that is Old Age."

Thor lifted his hammer to strike the fiercest blow yet, but the Giant King was not there. He spun round towards the stronghold, meaning to batter it down, but that too had vanished away.

The Twilight of the Gods

The Twilight of the Gods

THE most powerful of the gods was called Odin. One of his sons was Thor, the strongest of gods and men. Another son was called Balder. Balder was the noblest god that there was, and the one whom everybody loved best. He was the wisest and most merciful, the one who shunned all evil. He was so handsome and had such a noble expression that a sort of light seemed to radiate from him. His hair was bright and shining, and his skin was as white as the whitest flower that grows. Then a terrible thing happened, that made all the gods sad.

Balder was haunted by dreams that he was going to die. The gods decided that they must protect him from every possible

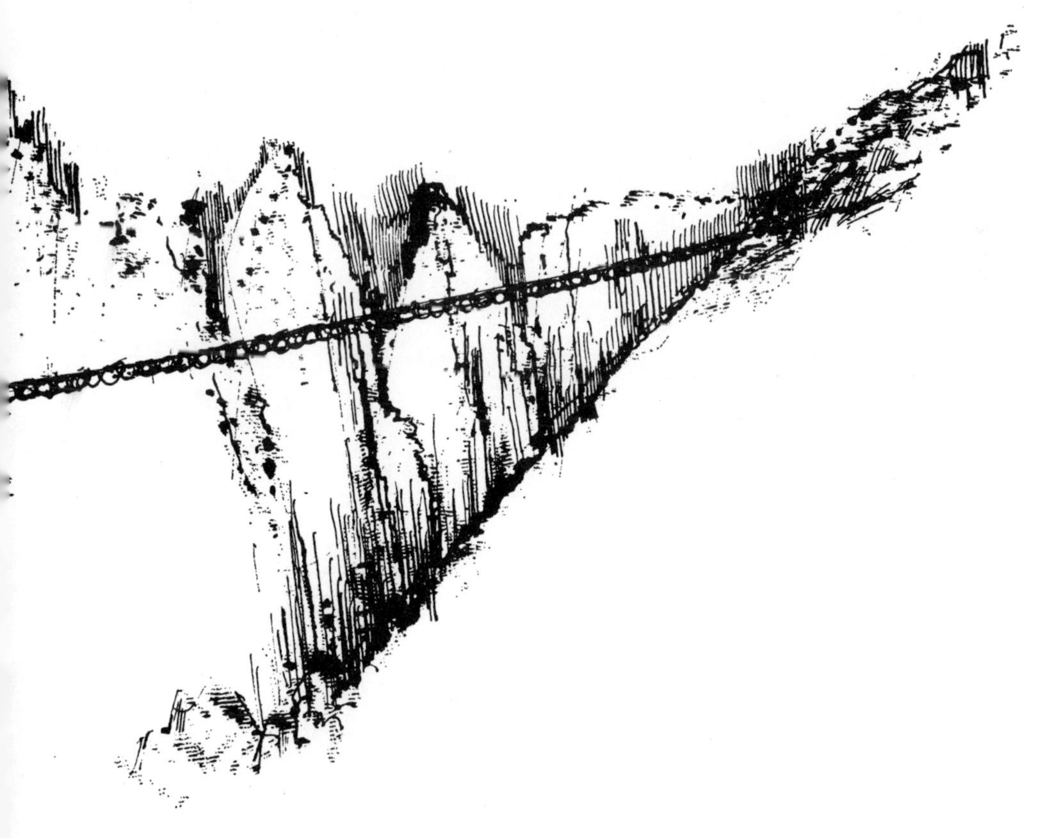

danger. The goddess, Frigg, his mother, made everything swear not to harm him: fire and water, iron and all other metals, stones, earth, trees, diseases, birds, beasts, poisons and snakes. When she had done this, the gods used to entertain themselves by hurling darts and stones at Balder. Nothing could do any harm.

Then one day, Loki saw them. Loki was handsome to look at, but he had an evil heart and was very cunning. He was always involving the gods in difficulties. Sometimes his cunning was able to help them out. When he saw Balder, whom all the gods loved so much, he was overcome by jealousy. He disguised himself as an old woman and went to see Frigg.

"I saw the gods throwing weapons at Balder, but nothing harmed him," said Loki, in a quavering old woman's voice.

"That is because everything has sworn me an oath," said Frigg.

"Is there anything you forgot to ask?

"Only a little mistletoe bush. It seemed to be too young to promise."

Loki went quickly to find the mistletoe. He broke off a sprig and took it to the assembly of gods who were hurling their darts at Balder. On the outside of the circle stood Hod, who was blind.

"Why aren't you joining the others?" Loki demanded.

"Because I can't see, and in any case I have nothing to throw."

"Go and join the others, and pay your homage to Balder. Here is a twig for you."

He took Hod's hand to direct his throw. The little dart of mistletoe flew through the air. It hit Balder and pierced a deep hole in his flesh. He fell dead. This was the greatest misfortune that had ever befallen the gods and men.

The gods were struck dumb with grief. They longed to take vengeance on Loki but could not, because they were in a holy place and dared not defile it. Odin was saddest because he understood best what a disaster it was. He knew that the death of Balder, might be the first tragedy that foreshadowed the doom of them all.

When they had recovered from the first shock, Frigg spoke. "Who will ride down to Hel, and try to bring Balder back?"

"I will," said Odin's son, Hermod. He jumped on to his father's charger, the finest of all horses, and galloped away.

Meanwhile, the gods carried Balder's body down to the shore. They launched his ship with its curved prow, and the whole world trembled. When Balder's wife saw the ship, she died of grief. They built a funeral pyre on the ship, and laid Balder on it with his wife beside him, and put on it a magic gold ring that was one of the gods' greatest treasures. Then they set it alight. All the gods came to see it, and the Valkyries who carry the souls of warriors slain in battle to heaven, and Odin's two ravens, as well as a great crowd of frost ogres and cliff giants.

This is what happened to Hermod, on his journey to Hel, the goddess who reigns over the underworld. For nine days and nights he rode through valleys so dark and deep that he could hardly see where he was going. At last he reached a bridge over a river, and rode across it.

"Who are you?" demanded the guardian of the bridge, when he came to the other side. "Yesterday, five troops of dead men rode over here, but the bridge resounds as much under you as it did under all of them together. You sound as heavy as a man who is still alive."

"I am looking for Balder," Hermod replied. "Has he passed over here?"

"Yes, I have seen him. Follow the road to Hel. It lies northwards and always downwards."

Hermod rode on till he came to the gates of Hel. The walls were amazingly high, and the gates were huge. He unmounted and tightened his stirrups, then got on his horse again and tightened his spurs. The horse jumped clean over the gate.

Hel, the daughter of Loki, was a terrible goddess, half black, half flesh-colour. Her hall was called Damp-with-Sleet; her plate was called Hunger; her knife, Famine; her bed was called Sick-bed; its hangings, Glimmering Misfortune. Hermod went into her hall, and there he saw Balder. He begged Hel to let him take Balder back.

"If everything in the world, both dead and alive, will weep for Balder, I will let him go back. If even one thing refuses to weep, I will keep him."

So Hermod returned, and the gods sent messengers all through the world, to ask for Balder to be wept out of Hel. All men and beasts wept for him. Even the stones and trees and all metals wept, just as you have seen them weeping on a warm day after the frost.

Last of all, the messengers visited a giantess in a cave.

"Will you weep for Balder?" they asked.

"I will only weep dry tears. He was no use to me, alive or dead. Let Hel keep him."

So Balder remained with Hel. The gods took a terrible vengeance on Loki, but it was no use. The death of Balder was the first of the great disasters that were to befall the gods. This is what would happen.

Winter would come, and last three years, with no summer in between. The terrible wolf, Fenrir, would break loose from his fetters, and would swallow the sun. Another wolf would swallow the moon. The stars would pour from the heavens, the mountains crash down, and the sea pour over the land.

The serpent coiled round the earth would spit poison into the sea and the sky. Fenrir would kill Odin. The gods would fight desperately against the wolf and the serpent, while the earth beneath them trembled and groaned. Then smoke and fire would leap up, burning the sky itself, and the whole world and everyone in it would be destroyed.

Afterwards, another world would rise out of the sea. It would be lit by another sun, the daughter of the sun which Fenrir had swallowed. Another race would live on the earth. Their food and drink would be the morning dew. They would bring forth enough children to people the whole world again.

That was all the gods knew about them.

The Curse of the Dragon's Gold

The Curse of the Dragon's Gold

THIS is the story of one of the Volsungs, the earthly descendants of Odin. No race of men was more fearless or more grimly determined. None was more famous or glorious, and none suffered more terrible things. The most famous of all was Sigurd.

Sigurd was born after the death of his father, Sigmund. Sigmund died as a Volsung should, fighting fiercely in battle. No ordinary enemy could defeat him, but Odin had decided that it was time for him to die, so he joined in the battle himself and broke Sigmund's sword. Without his sword, Sigmund was fatally wounded. After the battle, he lay on the field, dying, and his wife came out to find him.

"Take my broken sword," he said. "And make a new one from it. You are going to have a son. When he is older, he will do famous deeds with it. He shall be remembered as long as the world lasts."

The child who was born was called Sigurd. He was brought up by a foster-father, a dwarf blacksmith called Regin. Regin taught him many skills, how to speak different languages, how to write magic inscriptions in runes, and how to play chess. One day, Regin said, "You have not enough wealth for somebody of a noble race like the Volsungs. I will tell you how you can get more, if you are brave enough.

"I am one of three brothers. One of my brothers was killed by the god, Loki. At that time, my brother was disguised as an otter. Loki and Odin skinned the otter, and showed the skin to my father. He took them prisoner, and said he would only set them free if they would give him enough gold to fill up the otter's skin and to cover the outside as well. This was to be the price for taking my brother's life.

"To get this, Loki stole the gold which belonged to the dwarf Andvari. The treasure included a ring. Andvari put a curse on it, that whoever had the ring would die from possessing it. Soon, the curse proved true. My other brother, Fafnir, murdered my father to get the gold. He turned himself into a dragon, and now he lurks in the wilderness, guarding the treasure."

"Make me a sword," said Sigurd. "And I will kill the dragon and get the gold."

So Regin forged a sword. Sigurd tried it against the side of the anvil, and the sword shattered to pieces. He forged another, and once again Sigurd broke it. Then Sigurd went to his mother.

"Is it true that you have my father's sword, that was broken?"

She gave him the two pieces of the sword, and said, "You will win glory with this."

Sigurd took it to Regin, and asked him to make a new sword from the pieces. He did so. When he drew it out of the fire, it looked like a flame. Sigurd tried it on the anvil, and this time it was the anvil itself that was cut right through.

"Now go and kill the dragon Fafnir," said Regin.

"First, let me avenge the men who killed my father," said Sigurd.

He did so, and won great renown and glory.

"Now kill Fafnir," said Regin.

They rode to the desolate heath where Fafnir lived in the guise of a dragon.

"You can kill him as he crawls down to the water to drink," said Regin.

So Sigurd dug a great pit, and hid in it. The dragon lumbered towards the water. The earth shook under its heavy steps, and its breath poisoned the air. As it was crawling over the pit where Sigurd lay hidden, he plunged his sword into it, right up to the hilt. As he drew it out, he was drenched with its blood. The creature lashed frantically.

"Who are you?" it gasped.

"Nobody knows. I have no father or mother."

"You are lying."

"I am Sigurd, the son of Sigmund."

"You are going to take my gold from me, Sigurd. There is a curse on it. If you have that gold, you will die from possessing it. I know that my brother Regin has worked to bring about my death. You are only his tool and his dupe. He will cause your death as well. Take your horse, and ride away from here while you still can."

"I shall ride to your lair and take the gold."

"It will lead to your death, and the death of every man who owns it after you."

With those words, Fafnir died.

Then Regin came, and cut out the dragon's heart.

"Roast this for me over the fire," he asked.

So Sigurd roasted it on a spit. He touched it with his finger to test whether it was done. His finger was burnt, so he put it into his mouth to suck away the pain. As the dragon's blood touched his tongue, he found he could suddenly understand what the birds were saying.

"Sigurd should eat the heart of Fafnir himself. Then he will be wiser than all other men," said a nuthatch.

"Regin is plotting how to deceive him," another nuthatch replied.

"He should cut off Regin's head," said a third.

"Then he can have all the treasure himself," said a fourth. "After that, he can ride up to Hindarfell, where Brynhild sleeps. From her, he will learn great wisdom."

Sigurd lifted his sword, and struck off Regin's head. Then he rode to Fafnir's lair, and took away the treasure of gold and the ring that was said to bring death to whoever possessed it. After that, he set off on the long journey to Hindarfell. At last, he saw a tall cliff that seemed to be blazing with fire. He rode nearer, and saw that it was really crowned with a rampart of glittering shields. He made his way between them, and saw a young man in armour lying there fast asleep. He gazed down on him in astonishment, wondering who it could be. He lifted the helmet, and saw that it was a woman. He knew she must be Brynhild, of whom the birds had spoken.

She roused herself, and looked at him in a dazed way.

"Are you Sigurd, the son of Sigmund, who comes here with Fafnir's curse?"

"Why are you here?" he demanded.

"Because Odin put a spell on me. I am a battle-maiden whose whole joy is in fighting and in the clatter of shield and spear. Once in battle, I struck down a king to whom Odin had promised the victory. Odin said I should never win another fight unless I would get married, but I swore that I would not marry any man unless he was so brave he had never felt any fear. So Odin stabbed me with a thorn which put a spell of sleep upon me."

"You are wiser than any other woman," said Sigurd. "Tell me what I must do."

"Guard against loving another man's wife, and do not let your own wife's kinsmen hate you. Take care where you go, and take care whom you trust, for many men want to harm you."

Then Sigurd rode away. His shield and his coat of mail were all of a rich, reddish gold, and on his weapons was painted the terrible dragon Fafnir, to show all the world how Sigurd had vanquished him. His hair and beard were light brown, and his shoulders were broader and stronger than those of any other man. His eyes were so keen that hardly anyone dared to look him straight in the face. He was courteous and wise, and skilful in all the arts of war. Because he understood the language of birds, he was forewarned in all sorts of trouble. When the names of great warriors were remembered, he was counted the greatest of all. His name was known to every man who lived north of the Greek sea, and it will be remembered for ever.

After Sigurd had woken Brynhild, she went home to her foster-father. For the moment, she gave up her warlike deeds, and began to embroider a great tapestry. Although she had been a warrior, she was still more skilful than other women at peaceful work like this. One day, Sigurd was out hunting with his hawk. The hawk settled on a window high up in a tower, and would not come down. Sigurd climbed up to get it. He glanced in through the window, and there he saw Brynhild. He thought she was more beautiful than any other woman he had ever seen. Then he looked to see what it was she was embroidering with her gold thread, and saw it was a picture of his own wonderful deeds. He climbed down without her seeing him, and for the rest of the day he was very silent.

"Why are you so solemn?" asked one of his friends.

"I am thinking about Brynhild."

"A hero like you should not be so melancholy about a woman. In any case, Brynhild will have nothing to do with men. Her whole joy is in fighting battles."

Next day, Sigurd went to see Brynhild. He sat down beside her, and her women brought them great goblets of wine.

"You swore to Odin that you would not marry any man unless he was so brave he had never felt any fear. I am such a man."

He took her into his arms and kissed her, but she looked very serious.

"I am a warrior maiden. It is my destiny to help princes in battle. We shall never live together."

"If we have to be separated, that will be a pain sharper than any battle-wounds we have ever felt."

"You cannot change what we are fated to do. I must fight, and you must marry a king's daughter called Gudrun."

"I shall never love any other woman!" Sigurd exclaimed. "Swear you will love only me."

So they exchanged their vows, and he gave her the fateful ring from the dragon's hoard. Even as she was promising, Brynhild knew that he would never marry her.

Sigurd then went away, and soon after, Gudrun the king's daughter went to see Brynhild.

"I must tell you a strange dream that has troubled me very much."

"Oh, forget your dreams!" said Brynhild.

"No, I must tell you. I dreamed I saw a marvellous golden hart. Everyone wanted to have it, but I was the only person that it would come to. Then you shot it in front of me, and gave me a wolf-cub instead. It shook itself and spattered my clothes with blood, and I knew that it was the blood of my own brothers."

"If you really must know what this means, I will tell you. The golden hart is Sigurd, who has vowed to marry me. You will have him instead, but you will not keep him for long. Then you will be married against your own wishes to Atli the king of the Huns. He will kill all your brothers most brutally, and you yourself will kill him, and you shall welter in blood."

"I wish that you had never told me!" said Gudrun.

After that, Sigurd went to the hall of Gudrun's father. He talked so much about Brynhild that everyone knew that he loved her. Gudrun's mother wanted him to marry Gudrun instead, so she gave him a magic drink. After he had drunk it, he forgot all about Brynhild, and he married Gudrun. He gave her some of the heart of the dragon Fafnir to eat. He had carried it ever since he had killed the dragon. This made her wise, and also fierce and grim.

Then Gudrun's brother, Gunnar, decided he wanted to marry Brynhild, and Sigurd went with him to help to woo her. He had forgotten that once he had loved her himself. They rode a long way to the hall of Brynhild's foster-father.

"You will find her not far from here, in a hall with a golden roof," he said. "The hall is surrounded by flames. She has sworn she will only marry the man who is brave enough to ride through the flames to fetch her."

When they reached the hall, they saw the flames leaping up all round it. Gunnar urged his horse forward, but it shied, and whinnied with fear.

"Try my horse," said Sigurd.

But Sigurd's horse refused. Then Sigurd put Gunnar's armour on, and jumped on the horse himself. He dug his spurs into its side, and the horse leapt forward. There was a great rumbling, crashing noise, and the whole earth shook. The flames rushed up to the sky, then clouds of dense smoke swirled round him, so that he could not see. Suddenly, it died down, and he flung open the door of the hall. Brynhild was sitting there on a high throne, dressed in a coat of mail and a helmet. She looked like a swan on the crest of a rising wave.

"Who are you?" she demanded.

"I am Gunnar," lied Sigurd. "I have come to claim you as wife. I was told you had vowed to marry the man who would ride through the flames to fetch you."

Reluctantly, she agreed. He gave her a ring, and she gave him one in return. It was the same ring as Sigurd himself had given her when he had asked her to marry him, but he had no recollection of this, because of the magic drink. It was the ring he had had from the dragon's hoard, which the dragon had said would bring death to everybody who owned it.

Then Brynhild went home to her foster-father.

"What can I do? When I said I would only marry the man who would ride to me through the flames, I thought that no one would dare to except for Sigurd. He is the man I love."

"You will have to keep your oath and marry this Gunnar," he answered sadly.

So Brynhild and Gunnar were married. A great feast was held, and it went on for many days. During the feast, Sigurd suddenly remembered the vows he had made to Brynhild. But he was married to Gudrun, and now she was married to Gunnar. It was too late to do anything.

One day, after this, Brynhild and Gudrun went down to bathe in the Rhine together. Brynhild waded right out.

"Why do you go so far?" asked Gudrun.

Brynhild looked at her proudly.

"I do not choose that the same water that goes on you should go on me also. Your husband, Sigurd, is only a vassal.

Mine is the bravest of men, for he rode through the fire to claim me."

"You don't know what you're talking about. The man who rode through the fire wearing Gunnar's armour was really Sigurd himself. Here is the ring you gave him. It is the ring from the dragon's hoard. He gave it to me. Look!"

Brynhild went deathly pale. She hurried home, and would not speak a word for the rest of the day. Next time that Gudrun saw her she said in a malicious voice, "What ever's the matter? Surely you don't mind what I told you the other day?"

"Stop taunting me!" cried Brynhild.

"Why? You've got a noble husband. Better than you deserve."

"But you have married the braver man."

"Your husband, Gunnar, is wealthier."

"But Sigurd killed the dragon and rode through the flames. I value bravery far more than riches. And it was your mother who gave Sigurd the magic drink that made him forget that he loved me!"

After that, Brynhild went away, and brooded about how greatly they had deceived her. She would not eat or drink. Sometimes she lay in a feverish trance. Sometimes she became violent. She smashed up her tapestry which had the adventures of Sigurd embroidered on it. When Gunnar came near her, she shouted at him.

"I married you because I thought that you were the bravest of men. You were tricking me. It wasn't you who rode through the flames, but Sigurd."

Then Sigurd himself went to see her. She was asleep when he went in. She struggled to sit up, clutching the bed-clothes angrily.

"How dare you come? You have deceived me worse than

any one else. When you rode through the fire to me, I thought that your eyes looked familiar, but I could not see very clearly because of the haze that shrouded my destiny. Now, I don't want to live any longer, and the greatest of all my sorrows is that I cannot stain my sword with your blood."

"I was betrayed," protested Sigurd. "I didn't know you again because of the magic drink. When I remembered you, I loved you more than I loved myself. Forget your husband, and I will forget my wife, and let us think only of one another."

"I can never deceive my husband. It is not in my nature to profess love to two men at once. Go away, I don't want you."

Sigurd stumbled away. He breathed so heavily in his anguish that the links snapped in his coat of mail. Then Brynhild came to her husband, Gunnar.

"Sigurd has betrayed me!" she cried. "He has told the whole story to Gudrun, and she makes fun of me. I shall leave you unless you kill him."

So Gunnar very sorrowfully summoned his brothers together, all except for the youngest. They talked about what they could do. They stewed together the flesh of a snake and the flesh of a wolf. Then they called in the youngest and gave him this meat. When he had eaten it, he became cunning and fierce.

"Now go and kill Sigurd," urged Gunnar.

The boy was filled with a longing to murder. He crept into Sigurd's room, where he lay fast asleep, and stabbed him until all the bedclothes were covered with blood.

Sigurd raised himself up.

"It is Brynhild who has done this treachery. No man alive could have killed me in a fair fight."

With those words he died. Gudrun his wife wept, and Brynhild laughed aloud at her weeping.

"What a monstrous woman you are!" said Gunnar.

Then Brynhild burst into a terrible storm of tears and stabbed herself under the arm. A huge and splendid funeral pyre was built for Sigurd, and when it was blazing fiercely Brynhild crawled out and flung herself on it to die as well.

This is the story of one of the Volsungs, and of the ring which Loki stole from the dwarf Andvari. Andvari put a curse on the ring, and swore it would kill anyone who possessed it. First Regin's father had it, and he was killed by Fafnir. Then Fafnir was killed by Sigurd. Sigurd, who took the ring from Fafnir, was killed by the wish of Brynhild. Brynhild, who had the ring for a time, killed herself. Now Gudrun had it, and what lay ahead for her was as violent and disastrous as what happened to all the others. This was the curse of the dragon's ring.

The Water-Monsters

The Water-Monsters

PART ONE

HROTHGAR was a mighty king of the Danes, who had won great glory in battle. Young warriors flocked to serve him, and he soon had a large troop of fighting men. He decided to build a great hall where all his men could feast together. He gave orders for this to be done. Soon, the hall was finished. It was the largest and finest building that anybody had ever seen. He called it Heorot. Feasts were held in the hall, and the sound of revelry could be heard from a long way off: the noise of talking and laughter, and the clear, sweet sound of the minstrel's songs to the harp.

Everybody was glad to hear the warriors making merry, except for one. That was a creature called Grendel, an accursed monster who was doomed to live in the wilderness, cut off from men. He was bitterly jealous of all the joys in which he could never take part. One night, he slunk out of his desolate lair, and crept to Heorot under cover of darkness. The warriors were all laughing and making merry. He waited, crouched outside the hall, until they grew quiet and settled down to sleep. Then he swooped. He picked up thirty sleeping men and carried them off to his lair to kill them. The cruel and greedy creature exulted in the murder that he had done.

In the morning, a great cry of lament rose up from Heorot, when the outrage was discovered. Hrothgar was overcome by grief.

There was only a short respite. After one night, the monster committed more murders. He was so deeply steeped in sin that he did not feel any regret or shame. Then the great hall became deserted at night, for nobody dared to sleep there any longer. For twelve long years, Grendel harried Hrothgar's men, raiding and killing them without any mercy. He lay in wait for them on the misty moors. At night he would take possession of Heorot. They could do nothing to drive him away. They made many plans, which proved useless, and some of the Danes, in their folly, sacrificed to heathen idols. It was all in vain.

The story of Hrothgar's sufferings became widely known. It was heard by a very brave warrior in a neighbouring country. He was famous as one of the strongest men in the world. He decided to travel over the sea to offer his help to Hrothgar. Although he was very dear to his own people, they did not try to stop him from going, because they knew how great Hrothgar's need was. He chose fourteen bold warriors to go with him.

A ship was got ready and they went down to the shore. The ship lay under the lee of the cliff, and the sea eddied round her. The armed warriors went on board, and they set off. The ship breasted the sea like a water-bird, with the waves foaming round her prow. On the second day, they saw land, shining cliffs and broad headlands, and knew that they were at the end of their journey. They disembarked, and carried their war-gear over the gang-plank.

The mounted watchman, who was keeping guard over the cliffs, saw them coming. He saw the bright flash as the sunlight caught their shields. He was filled with apprehension as to who they could be, and rode quickly down to the shore. He brandished his huge spear.

"What armed men are you, who have come in a tall ship? I have kept guard on these cliffs for a long time, and I have never seen a warrior who looked more noble than one of you does. Tell me quickly who you are, and what you are doing here."

The leader replied, "I have heard stories of a mysterious enemy, who does terrible slaughter in the dark nights, and brings unbearable shame and distress to your people. I have come to see if I can help you."

"I accept what you say," the coastguard replied gravely. "I will bring you to see our king, and I will tell my men to guard your newly-tarred ship as she lies on the beach."

The warriors marched up the cliff path. The sunlight gleamed on their armour, and on their helmets which were covered with gold. The images of boars on their helmets gave them a fierce appearance, and their eyes glinted above their cheek-guards. They hurried on until they caught sight of Heorot, the greatest hall in the world.

"You can see your way now," said the coast-guard. "I must leave you and get back to my duties."

They marched on towards the hall. Their coats of mail, made out of a mesh of iron rings, clinked as they walked. When they reached Heorot, they rested their shields against the walls, and stacked their spears up together. As they were doing so, Hrothgar's herald came out to see them.

"Why have you come with all these weapons?" he asked. "You seem to be men of bold and adventurous spirits."

"My name is Beowulf," answered the leader. "I wish to speak to Hrothgar."

"I will ask him if you may do so," the herald promised.

He went in to the hall, where Hrothgar and his nobles were sitting, and approached the king formally.

"A lord from over the sea, called Beowulf, has come with his warriors. They would like to speak to you. I assure you that they all look like brave and noble men."

"I knew Beowulf when he was a youth," replied Hrothgar.

"I have heard of his reputation since, from sea-farers who have visited his own country. He is said to be as strong in battle as thirty other men. Perhaps God, in his mercy, has sent him to help us against Grendel. Tell them all to come in."

The herald went back to Beowulf.

"King Hrothgar told me to welcome you. Come in to see him, but leave your spears and shields outside the hall."

Beowulf told some of his men to stay outside and guard their weapons. The rest went into the hall, splendid in their helmets and cunningly-made armour.

"Greetings, Hrothgar," he said. "I have heard the story of Grendel's terrible deeds in my own country. Sailors have told me that this noble hall has to stand empty and useless every night, as soon as the sun has set. I have come to ask you if I may try to rid your hall of this monster. I will cast aside my sword and shield, and fight him bare-handed. God's will be done! If I am doomed to fail, Grendel will feast on my blood-covered body in some lonely spot, gloating over my death."

Hrothgar answered, "Thank you for your offer of help, Beowulf. I am glad to recall that I was able to help your father when I was a young man. It distresses me to tell you what Grendel has done to my people, and how my band of warriors is diminished. Many times, bold warriors have drunk a pledge that they would stay in the banqueting hall at night, and wait to fight Grendel with their terrible swords. Then, when daylight came, we would find the hall drenched with blood and my brave warriors taken away." He forced himself to seem more cheerful, and said, "Come and join in our feast."

A bench was cleared for Beowulf's men, and the great cup of ale was carried to them. A minstrel sang in a clear voice. There was revelry in Heorot. Only one man was not cheerful. He was called Unferth and he was jealous of Beowulf's fame.

"Are you the same Beowulf who held a swimming contest with Breca out in the open sea?" he asked in a mocking voice. "You risked your lives in the deep water, and Breca won. I don't expect that you will have much luck with Grendel tonight."

"You must have drunk a lot of beer before you dared to say that," Beowulf retorted. "Breca and I swam together in the fierce waves for five nights on end. He could not swim fast enough to get away from me. Then the tossing seas and the fierce north wind separated us. I fought off sea monsters with my sword, and my covering of chain-mail protected me from their bites. I killed nine of them. Then the bright sun rose, and the current bore me to the country of the Lapps. I have never heard any stories like this told about you, Unferth. If you had been as brave as you like to suggest, I do not believe that Grendel could have done so much damage in Heorot. He rejoices in killing, and takes no notice of you. But now I am going to show him what courage and strength really are."

The feast went on until darkness came. Hrothgar knew that Grendel would now be plotting how to attack the hall. He wished Beowulf good luck in his vigil, and he and all his warriors went off to rest, leaving the strangers to guard the hall. When he had gone, Bowulf stripped off his armour and handed it to one of his men.

"I am no less strong than the unarmed Grendel," he said. "Let God judge between us!"

He lay down to sleep, and his warriors lay down around him. They thought of all the men who had died in that hall. None of them ever expected to see his homeland again. At last, all those who were supposed to guard the hall fell asleep, all except one.

Then Grendel came from the mist-covered moor, striding under the clouds. When he reached the hall, he tore open the fastenings of the door with his bare hands. He strode on to the beautiful coloured floor and his eyes darted angrily round, like a lurid flame. He saw all the warriors huddled together in sleep. His heart was filled with joy to think that, before it was daylight, he could suck the life out of their bodies and feast on them all. As a beginning, he seized hold of a sleeping warrior and bit deep into his body. He drank the blood in his veins, and then he gobbled him all up, even his hands and feet. Next, he reached out his hand to another warrior who was lying as if he was sound asleep. Before he could take hold of him, his own hand was seized. He had never known such a strong handgrip. He wanted to flee back into the darkness, and slink home to his lair. As he pulled, the warrior stood up too. It was Beowulf. He gripped hold of Grendel's hand until he felt as if all the veins in his fingers would burst. Grendel tugged hard, and they swayed violently. They crashed into the sides of the hall. The benches were tugged from the walls, as they struggled together fiercely. If Heorot had not been so strongly built, they might have knocked it down.

The clatter was heard by all the Danes outside. Then they heard a more terrible noise, Grendel wailing loudly. The other warriors in the hall tried to attack Grendel with their swords, but their weapons were powerless against him. Beowulf hung on grimly. Suddenly, there was a horrible rending noise, and the monster's arm was dragged from its socket. Grendel stumbled away, the gaping wound spurting with blood, to die in his own lair.

So Beowulf cleansed Hrothgar's hall of the demon. The arm that he had wrenched off was left as a proof of this. People came from all the surrounding districts to stare at Grendel's arm, and nobody felt any shred of sympathy for him. The warriors rode to the lake where Grendel had had his lair. The water was turbulent and surging with blood from where the monster had died. They rode back joyfully, racing their bay horses on the sandy tracks, and praising Beowulf's daring.

At Heorot, Grendel's hand was displayed on the gold-covered roof. Hrothgar went in solemn procession to see it. He looked at the hand with its horrible claws that were as hard as steel, and thanked God that they had been saved from the monster. When Beowulf came back, he thanked him with great ceremony, and said that he would always look upon him as a son.

A banquet was prepared, and the hall hung with gold-embroidered tapestries to hide the damage where Grendel, in his struggle for life, had wrenched parts of the walls and doors apart. Everyone rejoiced and feasted. Hrothgar gave Beowulf valuable gifts of finely-wrought weapons and horses which had bridles plated with gold. Mead and wine were drunk freely, and the bard played on his harp and sang a stirring, heroic song. Hrothgar gave Beowulf more gifts of gold and precious jewels.

When it was late, Hrothgar retired to his rest. All the warriors settled down in the hall for the night, except for Beowulf who was taken elsewhere to sleep in state. Now, at last, Heorot was safe.

PART TWO

While they had been rejoicing, another creature was brooding about revenge. It was Grendel's mother, who was doomed to live in terror-haunted waters and icy streams. When it was dark, she came to the hall and crept in. The warriors started up and grabbed hold of their swords. There was no time to put on their armour. Before they could do anything, she had seized one of the men and escaped with him. On her way, she took Grendel's blood-covered hand from the roof.

Cries and laments rose up from Heorot. When Hrothgar heard the news, he was overcome with sadness. The dead man had been one of his most valued advisers. He summoned Beowulf and told him the terrible news.

"I have heard that there are two huge demons who haunt the moors," he said. "So far as people can tell, one of them is a woman. The other, a man, was the dreadful monster named Grendel. They live in a mysterious land of wolf-haunted slopes and windy headlands, of dangerous paths through the marshes, where the mountain stream plunges down into abysses of mist. Not far from here is a lake that is always shadowed by frost-covered trees. A terrible wonder is seen there every night, fire burns on the water. Nobody knows how deep the lake is. Even a hunted stag will turn and let the hounds tear him to pieces rather than try to save his life by plunging into that lake. If you dare to go and seek the monster out there, I will reward you again—if you ever return."

Beowulf answered, "Everybody must die sooner or later. The best we can do is to win glory while we can. I promise you that Grendel's kinswoman will never escape me, even if she hides in the depths of the woods, or plunges into the ocean."

Horses were saddled and they all set out. They rode along narrow paths and up steep, rocky slopes. At last they found the place, trees hanging over steep cliffs with blood-stained water below, and a fierce torrent plunging down into it. A terrible sight met them, the head of their murdered companion was placed at the edge of the cliff. They all grieved to see it.

The warriors blew their horns. The water monsters who had been swimming in the lake or lying on the rocks, dived back under the water in alarm. One of them was not quick enough, and Beowulf shot him with an arrow. The other warriors dragged out his floating carcase with their barbed spears.

Then Beowulf made himself ready. He put on his mail and his shining helmet, that was covered with gold and engraved with figures of boars. Unferth, the man who had taunted him earlier, lent him a sword. It had often shed blood in battle, it had never failed.

"I will either win death or fame with this!" exclaimed Beowulf, and with that he dived into the lake. He went down and down in the surging water. At last, he began to come up again. Suddenly, a hand grabbed him. Its horrible claws could not harm him because of his strong covering of linked chain-mail. He tried to draw his sword to fight his enemy off. He could not reach it, because there were so many strange beasts swimming about in the water, trying to break through his armour with their sharp tusks.

With a last strong tug, the creature who had seized him dragged him away from the water-beasts. To his surprise, he found himself standing on dry land on the floor of a cave. In front of him, was a curtain of rushing water. He had found Grendel's secret lair: behind the waterfall. He saw the bright gleam of a fire. By its light he could make out the huge shape of the woman monster who lived in the lake. He determined to kill her at once. His sword blade whistled through the air as he brought it crashing down, but the sword which had never failed in battle before, rebounded uselessly off her. Beowulf breathed deeply, and his resolution grew stronger. He tossed the sword to the ground, and vowed that he would trust to the strength of his hands, as he had against Grendel. He seized the creature by her shoulder to fling her angrily to the ground, but she clutched him so that he stumbled. Next moment, she was crouched on top of him as he lay on the ground. She drew her dagger and tried to pierce him to the heart, but his chain-mail saved him. He shifted his head and looked round. Suddenly, he noticed a huge old sword, hanging on the wall of the cave. He gave one jolt and broke free of the monster. He snatched up the sword, and, as she was trying to seize him again, he hit her furiously. The blade bit clean through her neck, and she crashed to the floor, with her head severed. Beowulf stood triumphantly, holding the blood-stained sword. He was out of breath from the fight, but he looked around resolutely. Then he noticed Grendel's dead body still lying there, with the terrible wound still gaping in his shoulder. He raised the sword, and cut off Grendel's head with one stroke.

The warriors, who were waiting by the shores of the lake, saw a stream of blood surge up through the water. They told one another sadly that Beowulf must be dead. Hrothgar and his men returned to the court. Only Beowulf's own followers stayed there. They were wretched, and never expected to see their leader again.

Down in the hidden cave, Beowulf stood with the sword in his hand. He stared at it in amazement as it started to melt away, like icicles when a thaw comes. Grendel's blood was so poisonous that it had destroyed the sword-blade. Only the hilt remained. He held the hilt in one hand, and seized Grendel's head in the other. He ignored all the treasures which had been hidden in the cave. Soon, he was swimming upwards. He swam on through the swirling eddies that had been purged of evil now that the monster was killed. He came to land, swimming strongly, and rejoicing in the spoils that he carried. His warriors shouted for joy to see their lord safely again. They took off his armour. The water was now growing calm. Then they started home. It took four of them to carry Grendel's monstrous head, and, even so, they found it difficult. At last, they reached Heorot, marching bravely and in a war-like fashion. They bore Grendel's head in triumph into the hall.

There was feasting and rejoicing again, and Hrothgar gave Beowulf more costly gifts. Then he sailed back to his own country. Several years later, the king and his son both died, and Beowulf became king. He ruled wisely and justly for many years. In the end, he died as bravely as he had lived, fighting a dragon which had been terrorizing the countryside. The dragon was killed, but Beowulf himself received a wound from which he soon died.

His men built a huge funeral pyre on the cliffs, and burnt his body on it. Dark smoke poured out of the pyre, and the roar of the flames mingled with the sound of women's voices weeping. Warriors on horseback rode round the pyre, lamenting their king. When the pyre was cold, they built a huge mound over it, and filled the mound with precious gifts and gold. The mound could be seen from far off at sea, to act as a landmark to sailors, and as a memorial to the bravest of kings.

The Giant's Daughter

The Giant's Daughter

Some of the names in this story are difficult to pronounce. As a rough guide, think of w *as* oo *(in Culhwch and Twrch Trwyth).* Ch *is pronounced as in the Scottish* loch.

THERE was once a queen who knew that she was dying. She had just given birth to a son. She did not want her husband to marry again, lest his new wife should treat the boy badly.

"Promise me you won't get married again until you see a two-headed briar on my grave," she said.

She did not tell him that she had made a servant promise to pull up whatever grew there. Soon after that, she died.

Every morning, for seven years, the king sent an attendant to look at the grave. It was always bare. At last, the queen's servant forgot to weed it. One day, when the king was out hunting, he went to look for himself, and found a briar growing there.

"Now I can get married again. I wonder who's the best person."

"I know a queen who would suit you perfectly," one of his counsellors said.

So the king went out to get her. She had a husband already, which was a bit inconvenient, so he killed her husband and carried the queen and her daughter off.

All this time, the king's son had been with a foster mother. It was not for a while that the new queen even knew he existed. When she heard about him, she had him brought to court.

"It's time you thought about getting married," she said. "You couldn't do better than marry my daughter."

"But I'm too young to get married," the boy protested.

His stepmother was annoyed.

"I'll put a spell on you then. No girl will look at you twice until you can win Olwen, daughter of Ysbaddaden Chief Giant."

All at once, the boy fell in love with Olwen, though he did not so much as know what she looked like.

"I'll tell you what to do," said his father encouragingly. "Go to your cousin, King Arthur, and tell him you want to marry Olwen, daughter of Ysbaddaden Chief Giant."

So the boy, who was called Culhwch, set off on a fine grey horse. The saddle and stirrups were made of gold, and he carried an axe so sharp it could cut the wind. Two greyhounds frisked round him, darting as quickly as swallows in flight.

When he reached King Arthur's court, he knocked at the gate.

"I'm not opening up," called the porter. "King Arthur has started his dinner, and you'll have to wait outside till tomorrow. We'll give you somewhere to sleep outside, and food for your horse and your dogs, and hot peppered chops for yourself, and a girl to entertain you."

"I'm not standing for this," shouted Culhwch. "I'll make such a noise that they'll hear me from Cornwall to Ireland."

"Make as much as noise as you like," retorted the porter. "I'm not letting you in, unless Arthur says that I can."

So the porter went off to Arthur.

"There's the handsomest man that ever I saw outside," he said, "and I've been all the way to India and to Africa and to Greece."

"Let him in," said Arthur. "We'll give him plenty to drink, and some hot peppered chops."

So Culhwch came in, and greeted the king.

"I have to ask you for something."

"I'll give you anything that you like, except for my ship and my sword, and my shield and my spear and my wife."

"I want to marry Olwen, daughter of Ysbaddaden Chief Giant."

"I've never heard of her, nor of her father. I'll send some messengers out to find her."

After a year, the messengers came back. They could not find Olwen anywhere.

"I'd better go home," said Culhwch.

"No, don't give in," said Cei, one of Arthur's knights. "I'll come with you to look, and if she really exists, we'll find her."

So they set out with five companions. They travelled until they caught sight of the largest fort in the world. For three days they walked towards it, until they me at shepherd.

"Who lives in that fort?" they asked.

"What! Don't you know? Ysbaddaden Chief Giant."

"We have come to look for his daughter Olwen."

"No one's ever done that and escaped with his life," said the shepherd.

He took them along to his house. His wife was upset to think what the giant might try to do to them. She opened a large box by the fire, and a boy with curly yellow hair scrambled out.

"It seems hard on him to be kept in a box," they said.

"That's because of Ysbaddaden Chief Giant. He's killed twenty-three of my sons, and this is the only one left. Why don't you all go away, before he knows that you're here?"

"Not till we've seen Olwen. How can we manage that?"

"She comes here every Saturday to wash her hair. I'll send her a message to come today, if you'll promise not to hurt her."

So Olwen came. Her hair was more bright than the flower of the yellow broom, anng d nothiwas as white as her skin, not foam on a wave, or the flowers of the marsh trefoil, or the breast of a white swan. Culhwch knew at once that he loved her.

"I must marry you!" he exclaimed.

"I've promised my father I won't get married without his permission, for when I get married, he'll die. You go and ask his permission. He won't give it, unless you promise to do all he demands. So promise, however unreasonable it seems."

They all went to the fort. To get in, they had to kill nine gatemen and nine watch dogs. Ysbaddaden Chief Giant was in the hall with his eyes shut.

"Here's Culhwch who wants to marry your daughter," they said.

"Where are those rascally servants of mine?" Ysbaddaden growled. "Lift up my eyelids so I can look at my future son-in-law."

The servants did so.

"Huh! Come back tomorrow," said Ysbaddaden.

With that, he picked up a poisoned spear and hurled it at them. One of them caught it and hurled it back. It hit Ysbaddaden on his knee.

"Curse you!" he shouted. "It's like the sting of a gadfly. It'll hurt me now whenever I walk uphill."

Next day, they went back again.

"Will you give your daughter to Culhwch to be his wife?"

"Not until I've consulted the rest of the family. She's got four great-grandparents still alive. I'll see what they think about it." With that, he picked up another poisoned spear, and hurled it at them. One of them caught it, and hurled it back. It hit Ysbaddaden in the chest.

"Curse you!" he shouted. "It's like the bite of a leech. I'll be short of breath now, whenever I walk uphill."

Next day, they went back again.

"Don't shoot at us any more, Ysbaddaden Chief Giant."

"Pull up my eyelids," Ysbaddaden called to his servants. "I want to look at my future son-in-law."

Next moment, he picked up a third poisoned spear and hurled it at them. This time it was Culhwch who caught it. He threw it back, and it hit Ysbaddaden's eye.

"Curse you!" he shouted. "It's like the bite of a mad dog. Now my eyes will water whenever I'm walking against the wind, and I'll get dreadful headaches as well."

Next day, they went back again.

"Culhwch wants to marry your daughter," they said.

"Let's have a look at him," growled Ysbaddaden.

Culhwch climbed on a chair, to get a bit nearer the giant.

"Now I'll tell you what you've got to do," said Ysbaddaden. "Get a cauldron from the overseer to the son of the King of Ireland, to boil meat for your wedding feast."

"That will be easy, even if you don't think so."

"You may do that, but there's something else that you cannot do. I must shave my beard for the ceremony. I cannot do that, unless you get me a tusk from the Chief Boar to shave myself with."

"That will be easy, even if you don't think so."

"You may do that, but there's something else that you cannot do. I must soften my beard before shaving it. I cannot do that unless you get me the blood of the Black Witch to soften my beard with."

"That will be easy, even if you don't think so."

"You may do that, but there's something else that you cannot do. I must comb my hair and cut it before I come to the wedding. It's so stiff that nothing is any good, except for the comb and shears that are between the two ears of a magic boar called Twrch Trwyth. He was once a king, but he was so wicked God turned him into a boar. He'll never let you have his treasures as long as he's alive."

"That will be easy, even if you don't think so."

"You may do that, but there's something else that you cannot do. You will never catch the magic boar called Twrch Trwyth until you can get a young hound called Drudwyn."

"That will be easy even if you don't think so."

"You may do that, but there's something else that you cannot do. You will never hold the hound until you can make a leash from the beard of Dillius the Bearded. It won't be any use, unless you pull the hairs out of his beard with wooden tweezers. He'll never allow you to do it while he's alive. And don't try killing him first, because that would make the hairs brittle."

"That will be easy, even if you don't think so."

"You may do that, but there's something else that you cannot do. The only collar that can hold the leash is the collar of Canhastyr Hundred-hands. You will have to get that."

"That will be easy, even if you don't think so."

"You may do that, but there's something else that you cannot do. The only man who can control that hound is Mabon, the son of Modron. He was taken away from his mother when he was three nights old. Nobody knows where he is, or even if he's alive. You will have to find him."

"That will be easy, even if you don't think so."

"You may do that, but there's something else that you cannot do. Mabon will never be able to hunt Twrch Trwyth unless he can ride on a horse called Dun-mane. You must get that as well."

"That will be easy, even if you don't think so."

"You may do that, but there's something else that you cannot do. You'll never kill Twrch Trwyth unless you can get the sword of Wrnach the giant. He'll never give it to you while he's alive."

"That will be easy, even if you don't think so."

"You'll never sleep at night while you are seeking these things. Come back when you've got them, and I'll give you my daughter. Except, you'll never come back."

They travelled all day until they saw another enormous fort. A black man, the size of three normal men, came out.

"Who does this fort belong to?"

"What! Don't you know? It belongs to Wrnach the giant. Nobody is allowed in, unless he is skilled at some trade, and nobody has ever come out alive."

They went to the gate and knocked.

"I'm not opening up," called the porter. "Wrnach the giant has started his dinner."

"But I'm skilled at a trade," replied Cei. "I know how to burnish swords."

"Then I'll go and ask Wrnach what he thinks."

"Let him in," said Wrnach, when the porter told him who was outside. "My sword needs a good polish."

So Cei went in all alone.

"Can you really burnish swords?" demanded the giant.

"Just you watch me," said Cei. He produced a whetstone and cleaned up half of one side.

"You're a very good workman," the giant said with approval. "What a pity you haven't a mate."

"My mate's outside. Why not let him in?"

Once more, the gates were opened. One of Cei's companions came in, and the others all slipped in after him. They got ready to kill Wrnach's men.

"That's a good job of work," said Wrnach when the sword was finished.

"It's your scabbard that's blunted your sword," said Cei, when the work was finished. "Let me show you."

He leant over the giant as if he was going to put the sword in the scabbard, but instead he plunged it into the giant's neck. He cut off his head with one stroke. Then he and his companions laid waste the fort. They got back to Arthur's court just a year after they had left. They took the sword of Wrnach the giant with them, because Ysbaddaden Chief Giant had told them that they would need it to kill Twrch Trwyth.

"What next?" said Arthur, when they got back

"We had better find Mabon, the son of Modron. He is the only man who can control the hound which is needed to hunt for Twrch Trwyth."

They set out again. One of them was an interpreter, who could speak the languages of birds and animals. They went to an old ouzel.

"Do you know where Mabon the son of Modron has gone to?" asked the interpreter. "He was taken away from his mother when he was three nights old."

"I have been here ever since I was a young bird," replied the ouzel. "When I came, there was an anvil here, and I have pecked at it for so long that it is now only as big as a nut. In all that time, I have never heard of the man you are asking for. I will take you to see a creature that is even older than I am."

He took them to see a stag.

"Have you heard of Mabon, the son of Modron, who was taken away from his mother when he was only three nights old?" asked the interpreter.

"I have been here since I was a young beast with only tiny antlers. I have seen a sapling grow up into a great oak-tree and then fall to the ground. In all that time, I have never heard of the man you are asking for. I will take you to see a creature that is even older than I am.

He took them to see an owl, and once again the interpreter asked his question.

"I have seen three woods grow up and fall down in this valley," the owl replied. "In all that time I have never heard of the man you are asking for. I will take you to see the oldest creature in the whole world."

He took them to see an eagle, and the interpreter asked him for news of Mabon.

"I came here a very long time ago," the eagle replied. "When first I came, I stood on a rock that was so high I could peck at the stars, but now it has worn down to the width of your hand. In all that time, I have never heard of the man you are asking for. I will take you to see a salmon. If he cannot help you, nobody can."

He took them to a salmon, and asked him if he had heard of Mabon, the son of Modron.

"I will tell you all that I can," the salmon replied. "There is a castle by the bend of the river. I have heard the bitterest cries I have ever heard in my life, coming from inside. Get on my back, and I will take you to listen."

So Cei and the interpreter climbed on the salmon's back. He swam up the river as far as the castle wall. They could hear a man lamenting inside.

"Who are you?" asked the interpreter.

"I am Mabon, the son of Modron. No man has ever been so cruelly imprisoned as I am."

They went back to Arthur, who set out with all his knights and attacked the castle. While the garrison was busy defending it, Cei broke through the wall by the river and took Mabon away on the salmon's back.

So they accomplished the second task of Ysbaddaden Chief Giant.

*

"What next?" said Arthur.

"We must find the only hound that can catch Twrch Trwyth."

They set out to find it. The hound was with its mother. She had changed herself into a wolf and was preying on sheep. They surrounded her, and took the young dog, and she changed into her own shape again. They went home with another task accomplished.

The next task was done by chance. Cei and a companion were sitting on the top of a mountain. The highest wind in the world was blowing. Below them, they saw a great column of smoke.

They went down to find out what it was, and saw, from some way away, a powerful-looking warrior roasting a wild boar.

"It is Dillius the Bearded. No leash will hold the young dog Drudwyn, except for a leash made out of this man's beard. It must be pulled out with wooden tweezers while he is alive. If we kill him first, the hairs will be too brittle."

"How are we going to do that?"

"Let's wait while he has a good meal, and then he'll probably go to sleep."

While Dillius was stuffing himself with wild boar, they spent their time making some tweezers. Soon after, he fell asleep. Then Cei dug a pit under his feet. He knocked Dillius into the pit, pulled out his beard with tweezers, and afterwards killed him.

Luck remained with them. In the course of some fighting, Arthur obtained the collar to hold the hound, and also the horse called Dun-mane for Mabon to ride on. Now they had the huntsman, his horse, the hound, its leash and its collar.

They also had the sword for killing Twrch Twryth. They still needed the boar's tusk, and the shears and comb from Twrch Twryth himself.

So Arthur went up to the north to kill the Chief Boar. His own dog brought the boar to bay, and not the dog Ysbaddaden had said would do so. They killed the boar, and pulled a tusk out of his head. Now they had the tusk for Ysbaddaden Chief Giant to shave his beard with.

They had got all these things, but still they needed Twrch Trwyth. Arthur sent a spy to find out if it was true that Twrch Trwyth had the shears and comb. The spy heard that Twrch Trwyth had already laid waste a third part of Ireland. He followed him there, and changed himself into a bird. He hovered over the lair of Twrch Twryth, and saw that the treasures were really there, in between his ears. He pounced, hoping to snatch them away. All that he got was a bristle, and this was poisoned, so that the spy was never well again for the rest of his life.

Next Arthur sent to Ireland to ask for the cauldron which belonged to the king's son's overseer. This was needed to boil meat for the wedding feast of Culhwch and Olwen. The overseer refused, so Arthur set sail for Ireland with a small force of men. They fought the Irish, and carried the cauldron off, together with other treasures.

They still had not caught Twrch Twryth. They found him in Ireland, with his seven young pigs with him. First the Irish fought him. They set their dogs on him from all sides, but they could not catch him. Next Arthur's men fought him. He hurt many of them, but they did him no damage. Then

Arthur himself fought him. He fought for nine days and nights, but all he could do was to kill one of the little pigs.

Then they sent the interpreter, who could speak the language of animals, to ask for the comb and shears. He went disguised as a bird.

"In the name of God, come and speak to Arthur," he said.

"We've got a grievance against God for turning us into swine," answered one of the little pigs. "Why should we help Arthur? Tell him he'll never get those treasures so long as Twrch Twryth is alive. And warn him it's his turn next. We're coming across to his country now, to see how much harm we can do."

So Arthur went back to Wales. Sure enough, Twrch Twryth and the little pigs swam over as well. Twrch Twryth ravaged the countryside, killing men and beasts. Whenever Arthur sent men out to hunt him, he killed the huntsmen. They managed to kill some of the little pigs, but still Twrch Twryth remained alive, doing more and more damage.

"This can't go on," said Arthur. "I'll catch him, if it kills me."

He gathered a great body of horsemen, and many dogs. Together, they managed to drive the boar into the river Severn. Mabon, the son of Modron, on the horse of Dunmane, rode into the river after him. So did Arthur and several others. They caught hold of Twrch Twryth and ducked him in the water. They held him under, while Mabon took the shears from him. Before he could get the comb, Twrch Twryth had managed to find the bottom beneath his feet. He heaved himself up, and dashed off, with the others in wild pursuit. He did not stop till he got to Cornwall. Two men were drowned, and many others were killed in an attempt to catch him again. At last they managed to hold him for long enough to get the comb, but, before they could kill him, he had pelted away. He dived into the sea and swam off, and nobody ever saw him again.

After all this, Arthur was very tired. When he had recovered, he said, "Is there anything else left to do?"

"We must get the blood of the Black Witch to soften the beard of Ysbaddaden Chief Giant, so he can shave it off."

They found the cave where the Black Witch lived, and two men went in to catch her. She seized one of them by the hair. The other grabbed hold of her, but next moment she had them both and was battering them on the floor. They staggered out, screaming and half dead.

"I'll have a try," said Arthur.

"It's not suitable for a king to go scuffling with an old hag," said his men. Two of them went into the cave. Soon they came out, in an even worse state than the others. They were helped on to horses, as neither could have walked home. Then Arthur himself went into the mouth of the cave. With his knife, he cut the old witch in two. They collected her blood. Now they had everything that Ysbaddaden Chief Giant had demanded.

So Culhwch went back to Ysbaddaden. The Giant's hair was cut, and his beard was shaved.

"May I marry your daughter now?"

"She is yours, but don't thank me for her. Thank Arthur instead. You would never have won her, if Arthur hadn't helped you. And now that my daughter is to be married, it's time for me to die."

So they took the Giant away and killed him, and Culhwch married Olwen. He never loved anyone else for as long as he lived.

And that is how Culhwch married the Giant's daughter.

Sir Gawain and the Green Knight

Sir Gawain and the Green Knight

IT WAS Christmas at Camelot and King Arthur was holding revels. For fifteen days, there was feasting all day, and dancing and music all night. Famous princes and beautiful ladies were gathered together there. The most beautiful of all the ladies was Guinevere, Arthur's queen. Rich food and drink were carried round, so that nobody ever lacked. The light from the banqueting hall spilled out on to the cold ground outside, and the noise of the revelry could be heard a long way off through the frosty air. But no one inside the hall thought of the world outside, their only thought was of feasting and merrymaking.

By New Year's Eve, King Arthur began to long for a change. His young blood surged through his veins, and his quick brain darted restlessly from one idea to another. He swore that he would not eat until something exciting had happened, or until he had heard some new and marvellous story. He sat drumming on the table with his fingers while the first course was served to the rest of his court. Then, suddenly, the great door at the end of the hall was flung open. A man on horse-back rode into the lofty hall. The banqueters laid down their food and the musicians stopped playing. They all stared at him in amazement. He was so tall that he seemed to be almost a giant, enormously strong, and yet supple and well-proportioned. The astonishing thing was, that he was green all over.

Everything about him was green, both himself and his clothes. His close-fitting coat and his mantle, his stockings and spurs were all green. His horse's harness was glittering with green stones. The horse's mane was as green as the knight's own hair, and his great green bush of a beard. He did not carry a shield, but in his hand was a cluster of holly, the tree that is green in winter when all the others are bare. In his other hand, was a huge axe of bright, shining steel, and that, too was a vivid green.

Still on his horse, he rode straight up to the King's table, that was on a dais at the end of the hall. He took no notice of anybody, and looked quite unabashed and fearless. Then he called out in a ringing voice, "Who is the lord of this gathering? I want to speak to him." He sat on his horse without moving at all, and looked them all up and down.

For a moment, nobody spoke. They stared at him in amazement, and marvelled how a man and his horse could be as green as the grass in the spring, or as bright green enamel inlaid in precious gold. Then Arthur said, very politely, "Welcome, sir, to our feast. Get down from your horse, and stay with us."

The Green Knight shook his head.

"I have come here because I have been told that you have the most valiant knights in the world, and also the most courteous. I have left my weapons at home and come to ask you to play a game with me."

"If you want to fight without armour or weapons, one of my knights will certainly fight you," said Arthur.

"Do you think that I want to fight beardless children like these?" mocked the Green Knight. He looked scornfully at all the knights in the hall. "I want a Christmas game. I will give this fine, heavy axe of mine to one of your knights. He can strike one blow at my neck, and I promise not to move while he takes his aim. I make only one condition. A year and a day later, he must seek out the place where I live, and I will strike him a blow in return."

They were more silent than ever, and sat without moving. The Knight stared them up and down. His eyes looked red beneath his bristling green brows. "What, is this Arthur's court, renowned for its bravery?" he cried in a mocking tone. He laughed wildly.

"Give me the axe," called King Arthur, and strode down towards him. The Green Knight leapt from his horse. He towered high above all the other knights in the hall. For a moment, everyone stared anxiously at the king, but still none of them had the courage to move. Then Gawain, the king's nephew got down from his place.

"May I take up this challenge?" he asked.

Everyone agreed that Gawain should challenge the Green Knight instead of the king. The king gave him his blessing and wished him good fortune. Then Gawain took the heavy axe and stood ready.

"We must repeat our bargain before we go any further," the Green Knight insisted. "Promise me, that in twelve months and a day, you will come to seek me out at the place where I live. You may be armed however you like, but you must come on your own. Then, whatever you do to me now, I will do to you then in return."

"I don't know where you live, or what you are called," demurred Gawain.

"That doesn't matter for the moment. If, after, you have hit me, I tell you where I live, you will be bound to set forth to keep your promise. If I never speak again, you can stay where you are now, without any dishonour. Now, let's see how well you can hit."

"Gladly," replied Gawain. He stroked the axe. The knight bent his head and his thick green hair fell forward to leave his neck bare. Gawain raised the axe up above his shoulders, and then brought it crashing down. It bit straight through the flesh and bone, and embedded itself in the floor beneath. The knight's head tumbled to the floor. Blood gushed out of his neck, and shone brightly on his green skin. The knight stood where he was, and hardly faltered or swayed at all. His severed head rolled about on the floor. Some of the onlookers made to kick it out of the way, but, before they could do so, he stooped down and picked it up. He vaulted on to his horse. Then he held up his head and turned it to face the dais. The eyes rolled from side to side, then, to everyone's horror, it parted its lips and spoke.

"Mind that you keep your promise, Gawain. In a year and a day, you must come to the Green Chapel, and there you will get a blow like the one you gave me. If you don't come, you will be known as a coward for the rest of your life."

With that, he rode out of the hall door. Sparks flew out from under his horse's hooves. At last, the onlookers found their tongues. King Arthur hid his astonishment. He managed to speak as though nothing disturbing had happened.

"Hang up your axe on the wall, so that everyone may wonder at it," he cried in a cheerful voice.

The feasting went on, and everybody was served with a double helping of food. The minstrels started to play again. Everyone talked and laughed. Sir Gawain joined in the feast and the merrymaking, but all the time he was wondering what was going to happen when he kept his promise to the Green Knight.

The year sped past very quickly. After Christmas came Lent, with its plain, sparse food. Then came the warm showers of spring, and flowers thrust through the ground. Summer followed, and all the hedgerows were rich with flowers. Soon, it was harvest-time, and when that was over, the winds of autumn started to blow. They wrestled with the sun in the sky, and tore off the leaves from the lime-trees. The grass turned grey and all the plants withered. Gawain watched all this, and thought of what he had promised to do.

He lingered at Arthur's court until the end of October. Then, on All Hallows' Day, King Arthur held another feast at his court. Sir Gawain went to the king, and asked his permission to go and seek the Green Knight. The king agreed, very reluctantly, that he ought to go when the feast was over.

Next morning, Gawain was dressed in fine armour that glittered and shone like the sun. He rode proudly away, and everyone at the court lamented.

"It is tragic to think what is going to happen to such a noble knight! He would have done better to have stayed here, instead of going off to be murdered by an enchanter."

Meanwhile, Sir Gawain rode far away, all alone except for his horse, Gringolet. At last, he came to North Wales. Anglesey lay on his left. He crossed over into the wilderness of the Wirral. He asked everyone whom he met if they knew where the Green Knight lived, but no one could help him. Now he started to travel through savage country, up steep hills and over fords where he had to fight enemies before he could cross. He fought against wolves and ogres who lived in the crags. But what was even worse, was the bitter weather. The cold clear water fell down from the clouds, and froze into hail before it could reach the earth. He had to sleep out among the bare rocks. The waterfalls thundered down from the heights and hung in icicles over his head. So he travelled, in great discomfort and danger, until it was Christmas Eve.

That morning, Gawain was riding through mountainous country. High hills rose up on each side. He rode through woods of huge oaks, and coppices of hazel and hawthorn tangled together. Rough moss hung from all the trees. The birds sang unhappily on the bare branches, and fluffed up their feathers against the cold. He prayed to Christ and to Mary that they would help him to find some shelter in that desolate place.

Suddenly the wood opened up, and he saw, in the distance, a castle which was surrounded by a large park. He hurried towards it. It was a fine castle of white stone, very well fortified. The drawbridge was up, so that he could not cross. Gawain looked at the woods behind him, and shivered. He called out, and a porter came.

"Please ask your lord if he can give me shelter tonight," called Gawain.

"Certainly," answered the porter.

He let down the drawbridge, and Gawain clattered across it. At once, he was surrounded by willing servants. They led Gringolet away to the stables, and took Gawain into the great hall. Then they heaped logs on the fire, and Gawain held out his raw, stiff hands to the blaze. His wet clothes steamed. Soon, the lord of the castle came out to greet him.

He was a huge man in the prime of life, with a reddish brown beard. He had a fierce-looking face and a commanding manner. He told his servants to lead Gawain to a bedroom. It was richly furnished. The servants took away his clothes which were sodden and dirty, and brought him some fine new, embroidered ones. Then they prepared a table and set food before him. They asked him where he came from, and he told them that he belonged to King Arthur's court.

The news that Gawain had come to stay, quickly went round the castle.

"Now we shall hear how they talk at court," said everyone happily.

That evening, Gawain met the lady of the castle. He thought she was even more beautiful than Queen Guinevere. Her skin was whiter than snow lying on the hills. With her, was an ugly squat old woman with heavy black eyebrows.

All that night they feasted, and Gawain talked to the lady. He was delighted with her company, but his manner to her was always courteous, not flirtatious. For three days they feasted, and then Gawain sought out the lord of the castle.

"Have you ever heard of the Green Chapel?" he asked. "I have made a promise to seek it out, and to find the Green Knight to whom it belongs. I must do so by New Year's Day."

The lord laughed. "You can stay here at your ease for another four days, and lie in bed in the morning for as long as you want to. The Green Chapel is only a couple of miles from here. Stay here and keep my wife company. I shall be going out hunting. Why don't we strike a bargain? Anything that I capture during the day, I will give you, and whatever you manage to capture yourself, you can give me in return. Come on, let's drink to it!"

The lord of the castle was up early next morning. He heard mass, and swallowed his breakfast quickly. Then he hurried off to the stag hunt, with his huntsmen and archers beside him.

Meanwhile, Gawain lay dozing in bed with the bright bed-curtains round him. Suddenly, he heard a rustling noise, then the curtains were drawn aside a little and a face peeped in. It was the lady. He pretended to be asleep. She crept inside the curtains. He opened his eyes as if he was very surprised to see her.

"Good morning," he said politely.

She sat down on the edge of the bed. She did not seem to have any intention of moving. Gawain looked at her doubtfully.

"I wonder if you could please go for a moment, so that I could get up and get dressed. Then we could talk better."

The lady laughed.

"We are all alone," she said in a beguiling voice. "The

men have all gone out hunting, and my waiting-women are all asleep."

Poor Gawain was in a dilemma. He wanted to get rid of the lady, but, because he had such a reputation for good manners, he wanted to do so politely. So he said in a non-committal way, "I am proud to be your servant," and he lay back and folded his arms.

The lady saw that he did not intend to move, so she lowered her eyes modestly and said, "I had better go." Then she looked at him through her lashes.

"Only one thing puzzles me, though. You told us that you were Sir Gawain. Even in these remote parts we know all about Sir Gawain. He is the most courteous of all King Arthur's knights. Everyone knows what beautiful manners he has. Surely Sir Gawain would not let me go without giving me a kiss. But perhaps you are somebody else."

Gawain, provoked by this, caught her in his arms and kissed her. Then she went, and he got up and dressed. The rest of the day, he spent with her and the ugly old lady who kept her company. They talked and laughed and enjoyed themselves very much.

All this time, the lord was out hunting deer. At last the moon rose in the frosty sky, the huntsmen blew their horns and they turned for home.

"See what I have brought you," the lord called to Gawain as he came into the hall. He showed him the fine stag which he had killed. "I have kept my bargain all right. Now, what have you won that you can give me in return?"

For answer, Gawain took him into his arms and kissed him.

"Where did you get that kiss from?" the lord demanded.

"That wasn't in the bargain," said Gawain. He laughed.

"Very well," said the lord as the wine was brought in to them. "Let's do the same thing tomorrow."

Next morning, the lord had leapt out of bed before the cocks had time to finish their crowing. He galloped away with his huntsmen and a pack of hounds ran beside them. The hounds streamed over the rocks which echoed to their cry. The huntsmen blew their horns or shouted them on. They found their quarry between a pool in the wood and a jagged cliff where rocks had tumbled down in confusion. All of a sudden, he rushed out. It was a huge wild boar with a bristling back, and dangerous, fierce-looking tusks. As he charged, he knocked three men to the ground, and the others scattered. Next moment, he had bolted off, with the hunt in pursuit.

All this time, Sir Gawain was lying in comfort. Once again, the lady visited him, and she talked to him about love. He answered her rather evasively, but he kissed her once. Then, as she was going, he kissed her again.

By now, the huntsmen had nearly caught up with the boar. He took refuge on a rock in the middle of a fast, swirling stream, and he turned at bay. His fierce eyes glinted and his wickedly-sharp tusks were lowered as if to charge. He was the most enormous and most murderous-looking boar that anybody had ever seen. He snarled viciously, and all the huntsmen drew back.

Then the lord leapt down from his horse, and waded into the stream with his sword in his hand. The bristles rose up on the boar's neck, and his breath came in a rasping growl. Everyone watched anxiously, terrified for the lord's life. Suddenly, the boar charged. It leapt on top of the lord, and they disappeared together under the fierce, surging water. For a moment, they struggled together there. The icy water snatched their breath away, and the current dragged them against the sharp rocks. Then the lord thrust his sword into the boar's throat, and deep into its heart. He dragged the dead weight out of the water. The huntsmen all blew their horns, everyone shouted with joy that the lord was safe, and the hounds bayed in triumph.

They carried the boar home. Everyone marvelled to see how enormous it was. The lord gave it to Gawain, and, in return, Gawain kissed him twice. He praised the lord's daring in killing such a fierce beast. The lady kept glancing sidelong at him, and he took great pains to treat her respectfully and courteously. He neither encouraged her nor rebuffed her.

All this time, the main thought in Gawain's mind was of what lay ahead. He took the lord aside, and said, "I must go in the morning."

"Why?" said the lord. "I promised you that it's hardly any distance to get to the Green Chapel. You'll have finished your business before some other people have finished their breakfast. Have another day's rest in bed. And let's keep on with that bargain of ours. I have tested you twice and found you faithful both times. The third time will be best."

Next morning, the lord set out again with his hounds clamouring round him. They sighted a fox and set off in pursuit. The cliffs echoed to their noise. Meanwhile, the lady had crept again into Gawain's room. She was dressed in her finest clothes.

"What, are you still asleep on such a beautiful morning?" she said.

Gawain was tossing restlessly in a dream of what lay ahead. He thought of the blow he would have to await in the Green Chapel, and muttered uneasily in his sleep. When he saw the lady, he roused himself to speak cheerfully to her. This time, her manner was more beguiling than ever, and he found it hard to know how to refuse her advances without appearing to snub her. She kissed him and offered him a ruby ring as a keepsake, but he refused it because it was too valuable.

"Will you refuse this then?" she challenged him. As she spoke, she took off a girdle of green silk, richly embroidered with gold, which she wore tied round her waist.

"I can't even take that," said Gawain. "I mustn't accept any gifts before I go to meet my fate at the Green Chapel tomorrow."

"Do you refuse my gift because it seems of so little value?" she teased him. "Let me tell you something. Whoever wears this green belt of mine is safe from his enemies. No one can possibly hurt him."

Gawain thought how thankful he would be to escape death at the Green Chapel. He took the girdle from her. She kissed him twice more and left, and he hid the girdle away.

It was nearly dark when the lord came home. This time, he offered Gawain the pelt of the fox, and Gawain gave him three kisses in return. He said nothing at all about the girdle that the lady had given him. All that night, they feasted and made merry. As they were getting ready to go to bed, Gawain drew the lord aside.

"You promised that you would ask one of your men to lead me to the Green Chapel."

"Of course I will," answered the lord.

Gawain thanked everyone for their hospitality, and went off to bed. His mind was very far from sleep. All night it was fixed on what might happen to him in the morning.

Morning came. The weather was wild. The sky was heavy with snow-clouds, and the shrill winds blew drifts of snow into every valley. Gawain lay in bed with his eyes shut tightly, but every time that he heard a cock crow he told himself that this was the appointed day. He was up before it was light, and dressed by a lamp in his room. He put on his finest clothes. Gringolet, his horse, was dressed in festive trappings. The bridge was lowered, and so he rode bravely out of the castle, with the man who was to show him the way to the Green Chapel. They passed by crags where the trees were bare, past cold cliffs and moors drenched with mist. Every hill was shrouded with clouds. The turbulent streams broke their banks as they swirled down with a spate of foaming white water. They twisted their way along, until, at the time when the sun should have risen, they halted on a hillside that was white with snow. The man who was showing Gawain the way looked round uneasily.

"The place you are so anxious to get to is not very far from here. It is a very dangerous place. The knight who lives there is the hugest man in the world, stronger than any four knights of King Arthur's court. He is a pitiless man who never shows any mercy to those who wander towards his chapel. Why don't you go home by some other way? I will go home, and swear by God and all his saints that you rode on towards the Green Chapel."

"I must go on," Gawain replied, "and see what fate has in store for me."

"If you really must go, ride down into that valley. You will see the chapel on your left hand. I wouldn't go with you for all the gold in the world."

With that, the man turned his horse and rode back towards the castle. Gawain spurred Gringolet on, and they picked their way down the rough hillside into the valley. When they were there, he looked round. He saw no sign of any shelter, only the hillside that rose up steeply and the gnarled rocky crags that seemed to graze the low clouds. He shuddered at the desolate place. Then he noticed a little hillock of ground, beside the swollen stream that rushed through the valley. He rode towards it, and tethered Gringolet to the branch of a tree. He walked round it doubtfully. From nearer to, the hillock now looked like a cave overgrown with grass. Could this be the Green Chapel?

"It's only fit for the devil to say his prayers in at dead of night!" he exclaimed. "How desolate it is! What an accursed place!"

All of a sudden, he heard a noise. It sounded like someone sharpening a scythe on a grindstone. The noise echoed round the cliffs, as loud as the rush of water through a mill-race.

"This is something being prepared for me," thought Gawain. "Well, I won't be afraid of a noise." He called out loudly, "Who is here? Gawain is ready to meet you, whoever you are."

"Wait," called a voice. "In a moment you shall have what I promised you." With that, the Green Knight appeared on the other side of the water. He was dressed as he had been before, and was holding an axe in his hand. He leapt over the water, using his axe as a stick.

"I see you can keep your promises," he said to Gawain. "Now we are here in this valley, I will repay you for what you did to me a year and a day ago. Take off your helmet, and don't delay. I didn't delay last year when I let you swipe my head off with one stroke."

Gawain bowed down his head with the bare skin of his neck exposed. He tried to pretend not to care. The man in green made to get ready to hit. He raised up the axe with all the strength in his mighty body. Gawain glanced sideways, and when he saw the glint of the axe, he shivered a little.

"What, are you the famous Gawain?" mocked the Green Knight.

"I flinched once," Gawain replied. "But I won't again. Remember, though, that if my head rolls to the ground, I can't restore it as you did. Hurry up, and do whatever you have in store for me."

"Have at you, then," the Green Knight shouted. He raised his axe high. Gawain stood without moving a muscle, as firm as a stump with a hundred roots in the rocky ground.

Then the Green Knight spoke again in his mocking voice.

"Cover your head with your hood. Perhaps that will save you."

"Go on!" shouted Gawain furiously.

"Very well, here you are," cried the Green Knight, and with that he brought his axe crashing down onto Gawain's neck. The blow was powerful, and yet it only bit through the skin. The bright blood ran on to Gawain's shoulders and spattered on to the snow. When he saw it, he leapt for joy to know himself still alive. He had never been so happy since the day he was born.

He snatched up his sword and called, "Stop your blows. I have taken one hit from you, as we promised in Arthur's court. If you hit me again, I am going to fight back."

The Green Knight leant on his axe. He spoke merrily, with a ringing voice.

"Don't be so angry, Gawain. The first time I raised my axe it was only pretence, in memory of the time when you made me a promise and kept it. You gave me all that you won during my first day's hunting. The second time was only pretence as well, in memory of the next time you kept your promise. But the third time, I hit you a little, because, the third time we made a bargain, you played me a little false. You never gave me my own green belt which you had from my wife."

Then Gawain realized that the Green Knight was the same as the lord of the castle. He felt very ashamed as he pulled the girdle from its hiding place, and offered it to the lord.

"Keep it," the lord cried cheerfully, "as a memory of our encounter. You are a brave knight, Gawain."

"Tell me one thing before I go," Gawain demanded. "What is your real name?"

"Bercilak de Hautdesert," the Green Knight replied. "All that has happened is through the skill of Morgan le Fay, the enchantress. She is the ancient lady who lives in my house. She planned this because she hates Queen Guinevere, and because she expected that it would be Arthur himself, and not one of his knights, who would take up the challenge. You have acquitted yourself bravely. I wish you a safe journey home."

So Gawain rode back to King Arthur's court. In spite of the Green Knight's praise, he felt shame at what he had done. When he reached the court, he was greeted with joy by Arthur and all his knights. He told them the story of what had happened and vowed that he would always wear the green belt as a token of his shame. But the knights followed his fashion, and all wore a bright green sword-belt, in memory of how bravely Gawain had kept his word.

"In You my Death, in You my Life"

"In You my Death, in You my Life"

THE hero of this story is called Tristan. He was born in France, and his name comes from the French word *triste,* meaning sad. It is a very suitable name, for this is a sad story.

When Tristan was born, his mother died. His father, whom she had loved greatly, had been killed shortly before. Fortunately for the orphan baby, his father had a very loyal friend called Rual, who had been left in charge of his lands. Rual and his wife took Tristan into their own home, and brought him up as their son. They loved him at least as much as their own children. They were very proud of him too. As Tristan grew up, he learnt all the things that a boy ought to know about fighting and hunting, but as well as this, he became a skilful musician and was gifted at speaking foreign languages.

One day, a ship from Norway put into harbour near Tristan's home. He went on board, for he had been told that the men had some falcons for sale. He started to play chess with some of the merchants on board. They were amazed at his skill. They persuaded him to sing, and to speak different languages for them. Then, while he was playing chess, they set sail again. They thought that they might exploit Tristan's cleverness for their own gain. When the servant, who was with Tristan, protested, they set him adrift in an open boat.

Then a terrible storm arose. It raged for eight nights and days. The merchants decided it must be a punishment to them for stealing Tristan away. They put him ashore on the nearest coast, which happened to be Cornwall. Tristan did not know, but his mother, who had died when he was born, had been the sister of King Mark of Cornwall. She had eloped with his father, and nobody in Cornwall had any idea what had become of her.

Poor Tristan was wretched at being abandoned like this. By a fortunate chance, King Mark was hunting nearby. Some of his huntsmen got into conversation with Tristan. They were very impressed indeed at how much he knew about hunting, and how well-spoken he was. They took him to see the King. He had no idea at all that the boy was really his nephew, but he liked him, and felt sorry for him, and took him back to his castle. Soon, Tristan became a general favourite. Everyone was astonished at how gifted he was, although he was only fourteen. He could ride well, and play many musical instruments, and speak many different languages. He was also very good-looking. Nobody felt jealous of him, however, because he was so courteous and unassuming.

For nearly four years, Tristan lived at King Mark's castle, Tintagel. Then a stranger came to the castle. It was Rual, Tristan's foster-father, who had been seeking his beloved son ever since he had disappeared. He looked shabby and old and exhausted, because he had travelled so far, but Tristan was overjoyed to see him. When Rual saw how happy Tristan was at Tintagel, and how much King Mark loved him, he at last revealed the secret of who the boy really was. He proved it to King Mark by showing him a ring that had belonged to Tristan's dead mother, his sister. Mark vowed that he would always love Tristan as his own son.

When he knew who he really was, Tristan decided to throw in his lot with Mark. He rewarded the loyal Rual with the overlordship of his own lands in France. Rual accepted very reluctantly.

At this time, a terrible sorrow befell Cornwall. The King of Ireland demanded tribute from them. The first year, he had asked for bronze, the next year for silver, and after that, gold. Now, he was asking for something far more precious, their own sons. His messenger was a man called Morold, the Queen of Ireland's brother. Morold was a fierce and terrible fighter, and everyone was afraid of him. Tristan was roused by how meekly the Cornish gave in to Morold, and challenged him to single combat. He had no experience in such desperate fights, and everyone took it for granted that he would be killed.

A battle-ground was appointed, a little island within easy sight of the shore. The two men went there alone. Soon Morold was fighting so fiercely, that Tristan would have been killed except for the skill with which he defended himself with his shield. Then Morold got behind his guard and gave him a terrible wound in the thigh.

"You will die of this, Tristan," he shouted. "Nobody in the whole world can help you, except for my sister, the Queen of Ireland. If you will surrender and give me the tribute I ask for, I will get her to help you."

"I will never surrender," cried Tristan. With a desperate rush, he attacked Morold again, and struck his head with his sword. It was a death-blow. The exultant Cornish took Morold's dead body and sent it back to Ireland.

"This is the only tribute we will pay to Ireland," they said.

Nobody knew that in Morold's skull was a fragment of Tristan's sword.

Everybody rejoiced that Morold had been killed, but Tristan himself could take no part in their celebrations. The wound in his thigh festered and he became more and more ill. As he tossed feverishly, Morold's words kept on coming into his mind.

"Nobody in the whole world can heal you except for my sister, the Queen of Ireland."

How could he go to Ireland and ask for help from the woman whose brother he had killed? Yet, if he did not go, he would certainly die. At last, he decided to take a desperate course. He would go to Ireland, in disguise.

He did so. When his ship was near the Irish coast, he told his companions to dress him in shabby clothes and to set him adrift in an open boat, with a harp and a supply of food. They did so, and sailed away. Some men from Dublin saw him and took him to land. Tristan told them that he was a minstrel whose ship had been attacked by pirates. In spite of his serious illness, he played and sang so sweetly that they were enchanted. Soon, a report of this gifted musician had reached the Queen, and she asked for him to be brought to her. She examined his wound.

"Your leg is poisoned," she said, "but I promise you I can heal it. Then, when you are better, you can teach some of your skill at music to my daughter, Iseult."

So the Queen lavished all her great skill and learning on curing Tristan. If she had known who he was, she would have killed him instead, in revenge for her brother's death, but she thought he was just a minstrel. He had told her his name was Tantris. When he had recovered, he started to teach Iseult. He taught her music, and also read books with her, and instructed her in the arts of courtly behaviour and fine manners. She became a most charming and highly accomplished girl. She had always been beautiful. At last, when he was really well, he said he must return home. The Queen was very reluctant to let him go, but he pretended he had a wife waiting for him.

When Tristan got back to Cornwall, everyone was anxious to hear about his adventures. They were especially interested in his stories about the beautiful girl, Iseult. King Mark's advisers urged him to marry her, to provide an heir to the throne.

"I will never get married," Mark replied. "Tristan is my heir."

But Tristan himself urged his uncle to marry. He was afraid that Mark's courtiers might murder him, they had become so jealous of all his achievements. He even offered to go to Ireland to woo her for Mark. This was a very dangerous undertaking, as the Cornish and Irish were on such bad terms with each other.

So, once again, Tristan landed in Ireland in disguise. He had a plan. There was a terrible dragon that was laying waste the country. The King had promised to give his daughter to anybody of noble birth who could kill it. Tristan armed himself for the fight. He attacked the dragon, and after a terrible struggle, killed it. He just managed to cut out its tongue before he collapsed, overcome by the dreadful fumes of the dragon's poisonous breath.

Now things began to go wrong. The King's Steward found the dead dragon and cut off its head. He claimed that he should marry Iseult. The poor girl was horrified at the prospect. Fortunately, her mother, the Queen, had a dream that the dragon had really been killed by a stranger. She went to the place and found Tristan's unconscious body. She took him home to her palace, and for the second time, she nursed him back to health. She was delighted when she recognized her friend, the supposed Tantris. Then another misfortune happened. Young Iseult was very curious about Tantris. His behaviour was so noble that she found it hard to believe he was only a minstrel. One day, she looked through his armour in search of a clue as to who he really was. She found his sword with a piece of metal missing. In alarm, she fetched the splinter that had been taken out of her uncle's skull. It fitted perfectly. At once, everything was clear. His name Tan-tris was really Tris-tan: her uncle's slayer.

In her horror, she nearly killed him with his own sword, but was seized by pity at the last moment. Her mother also was aghast when she heard the news. They wondered whether they should have him executed for killing Morold. One thing stopped them, the fact that only he could destroy the Steward's pretensions to marry Iseult. And so he did. When the Steward produced the dragon's head as proof of his claim to marry Iseult, Tristan challenged him to produce the tongue. When he could not, Tristan did so, and the Steward retired in disgrace.

Now Tristan was in a commanding position. He was officially forgiven for killing Morold. As his reward for killing the dragon, he claimed Iseult's hand on behalf of his uncle, King Mark. This was granted, and a treaty of friendship between the two countries was made. Tristan and Iseult got ready to sail for Cornwall. Except that Iseult still resented Tristan's having killed her uncle, all seemed to be well. The succession of misfortunes which had overtaken Tristan since his unhappy birth might be at an end at last. He did not know that the worst misfortune was still to come.

The Queen was determined her daughter should live happily with King Mark. She used all her skill to make a love potion, and gave it to her niece, Brangane, who was to go with Iseult.

"The two who drink this potion together will love one

another for the rest of their lives. Nobody else will ever matter to them. Take care that nobody touches it, except for my daughter and Mark."

They set sail. Iseult would still barely speak to Tristan. The journey was rough and Tristan put into a haven for the sake of the ladies on board. He went into Iseult's cabin to see how she was. He asked for a drink, and one of her ladies-in-waiting, a very young girl, who was there, gave both Tristan and Iseult some of the love-potion out of a flask. Brangane came in at this moment. She seized the flask and hurled it into the sea, but she was too late, they had drunk the potion already.

From that time, what the Queen had foretold came true. The two who had drunk that potion loved one another for the rest of their lives. They tried to struggle against their love, but it was in vain. Iseult was married to Tristan's uncle, but still they loved one another. At first, Mark suspected nothing, but gradually his courtiers, who had long been jealous of Tristan, put doubts into his mind. Iseult managed to set aside his fears. Several times, Mark tried to trick her into revealing the truth, but she cleverly managed to make his suspicions seem nonsense. Mark loved her so much that he was only too anxious to be persuaded she loved him in return.

But this could not go on for ever. Tristan and Iseult loved one another so strongly that their love was like a fierce wind that destroys everything in its path. In spite of Iseult's evasions, Mark became suspicious again, and for a time he banished them both from the court. Then he let them return. Iseult was so beautiful and so charming that it was easy for him to persuade himself that he was wronging her. All the same, he warned her never to see Tristan alone, for the sake of her reputation. Iseult found this very hard to endure. The love that she felt for Tristan burnt her up like a fire. One day, she sent him a message to meet her out in the orchard. There King Mark spied them, clasped in each other's arms. As soon as he realized he had seen them, Tristan fled from the country to avoid certain death.

His life in Cornwall was ruined, and he went back to his own country. The loyal Rual was dead, but Rual's sons greeted him gladly. Now Tristan had to make a new life for himself. All the time he was wracked by the fever of love with which the potion had infected his blood. His friends hoped that he would marry the princess of a neighbouring country, called Iseult of the White Hands. They were encouraged because, whenever he sang to the harp, he would bring in the same refrain,

Iseult ma drue, Iseult ma mie,
En vous ma mort, en vous ma vie.

That is to say:

Iseult my love, my heart's dear wife,
In you my death, in you my life.

Everyone thought that he meant Iseult of the White Hands, including the girl herself. At last, he decided to marry her. She was beautiful and she loved him, and she had a name that he delighted to say. Perhaps she would help him to forget Iseult of Ireland.

He married her, and soon realized how useless it had been. He was cold and distant to his poor wife, and his love for the other Iseult obsessed him more than ever. Nothing could free him from the effects of the love potion, except for death itself. This was nearer than he knew. He promised a knight to help him regain his lady who had been carried off to an enemy's castle. In the fighting, the knight was killed, and Tristan himself was severely wounded. Once again, he had come to grief through circumstances that were none of his own fault. His wound became infected and it was obvious that he might die. He felt that only one thing could save him, and that was to see his beloved Iseult again.

He asked a messenger to go to Cornwall to seek her.

"If you bring her back with you, put white sails on your ship so that I shall know. If she cannot come, put on black sails."

While he was speaking, his wife, Iseult of the White Hands, had been listening and had heard every word that he said.

The messenger went to King Mark's court, and Iseult agreed to go to Tristan. She stole away in the darkness. They sailed for Brittany. All this time, Tristan had been keeping himself alive, simply by his longing to see Iseult.

At last, the ship which was bringing her drew near to shore. Tristan's wife, Iseult of the White Hands, was watching from the window. She saw a ship with white sails, and plotted about what to do.

"I see a ship coming," she said. "All the sails are black."

With that, Tristan gave up the struggle to live. He died of his disappointment. When Iseult landed, she heard the bells tolling for his death. She hurried up to the palace, and took his dead body in her arms. Then she, too, died of her grief. They had found their death in each other, as once they had found their life.

The Werewolf

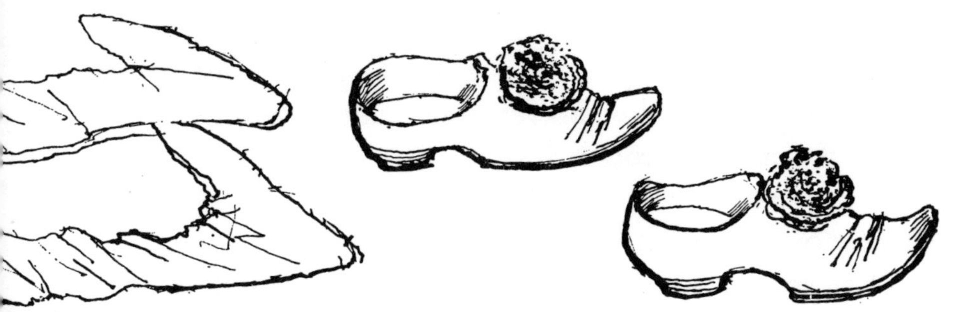

The Werewolf

IN EVERY country, there are stories about werewolves, creatures which have the outward appearance of men, but which change into wolves at night. Here is a story from Brittany.

There was once a nobleman who was very well thought of by everyone, including the king of his country. His wife loved him dearly. Only one thing upset her, for three days every week he would go away. Nobody knew where he went.

One day, when he came back from one of his absences, she said to him, "Please will you grant me a wish?"

"I will do anything for you," he said affectionately.

"Tell me where you go to when you disappear. I am dreadfully worried about it."

"For God's sake, don't ask me that. If you knew, you would never love me again."

She thought that he must be joking, and once again begged him to tell her. At last he yielded.

"I turn into a wolf. I go into the depths of the forest, and there I live on roots and whatever prey I can capture."

"What about your clothes?"

"When I am a wolf, I don't need them."

"What do you do with them, then?"

"I can never tell you. If anyone stole my clothes, or even saw me taking them off, I would have to remain a wolf for ever."

"But you know that I would never betray you," she said. She went on pleading, and, in the end, he told her.

"In the wood, a little way from the path, there is an old chapel. I have often gone there to lament the fate that has made me a werewolf. Nearby, is a hollow stone, hidden by a bush. That is the hiding place for my clothes."

When she heard this story, the lady was terrified. She felt that she dare not live with him any more. She wrote to a knight who had long admired her, to ask his help. She had never before given him any encouragement, but now she asked him to go to the hollow stone and steal her husband's clothes. He did so, and now her husband could not turn back to a man again. Everyone wondered where he had gone. After a time, she and the knight got married.

More than a year later, the king was out hunting in the wood where the werewolf lurked. The hounds got his scent, and chased him. They had caught up with him, and would soon have torn him to pieces, if he had not run up to the king and taken his stirrup between his paws. He gazed up at him imploringly.

"This wolf can nearly speak," said the king. "Watch him asking for mercy. I will take him back to my castle."

From that day, the wolf lived in the castle, like a favourite dog. The king would never part with him. Listen to what happened next.

One day, the king held a feast, and invited all the chief men in his country to it. One of them was the knight who had married the werewolf's wife. The moment he entered the hall, the werewolf pounced on him. He would have bitten him badly, if the king had not intervened. The wolf attacked the knight twice again. Everyone said how unlike him it was to be fierce. They thought that the knight must have done him some injury in the past, but nobody knew what it was.

Not long afterwards, the king went out hunting. He happened to meet the lady who had once been the werewolf's wife. At once, the werewolf became almost demented. He sprang at her savagely. The king's men hauled him off, and nearly beat him to death with their swords. One of the counsellors stopped them, and spoke to the king.

"There must be something behind this. The wolf is gentle to everyone, except for this lady and her husband. You remember her first husband, sire? He was a close friend of yours, and now he has disappeared, and nobody knows what has happened to him. Suppose you have the lady questioned, and see if she knows why the wolf should hate her so much."

So the lady and her knight were taken away and questioned. In the end, she revealed what had happened. She told them how her husband's clothes had been stolen away from the hollow stone. She did not know where he had gone, but in her heart, she was convinced that he was the wolf.

At once, the king ordered the lord's clothes to be brought. He had them spread out before the wolf, but the wolf took no notice at all. Then the wise counsellor spoke again.

"The wolf may be ashamed to turn back into human shape in front of us all. Take him somewhere private, and leave him there with his clothes. Then we will go back later and see what has happened."

The king took the wolf to his own room, and shut the

doors on him. A little later, he looked in again. He saw the lord, his friend who had been lost, lying on the bed, sleeping as peacefully as a child. He greeted him with delight.

Then the king restored his lands to the lord, and gave him many precious gifts. He banished his former wife and her new husband from the kingdom.

Now, this is not a story made up for entertainment. It happened just as I said.

The Battle in the Pass

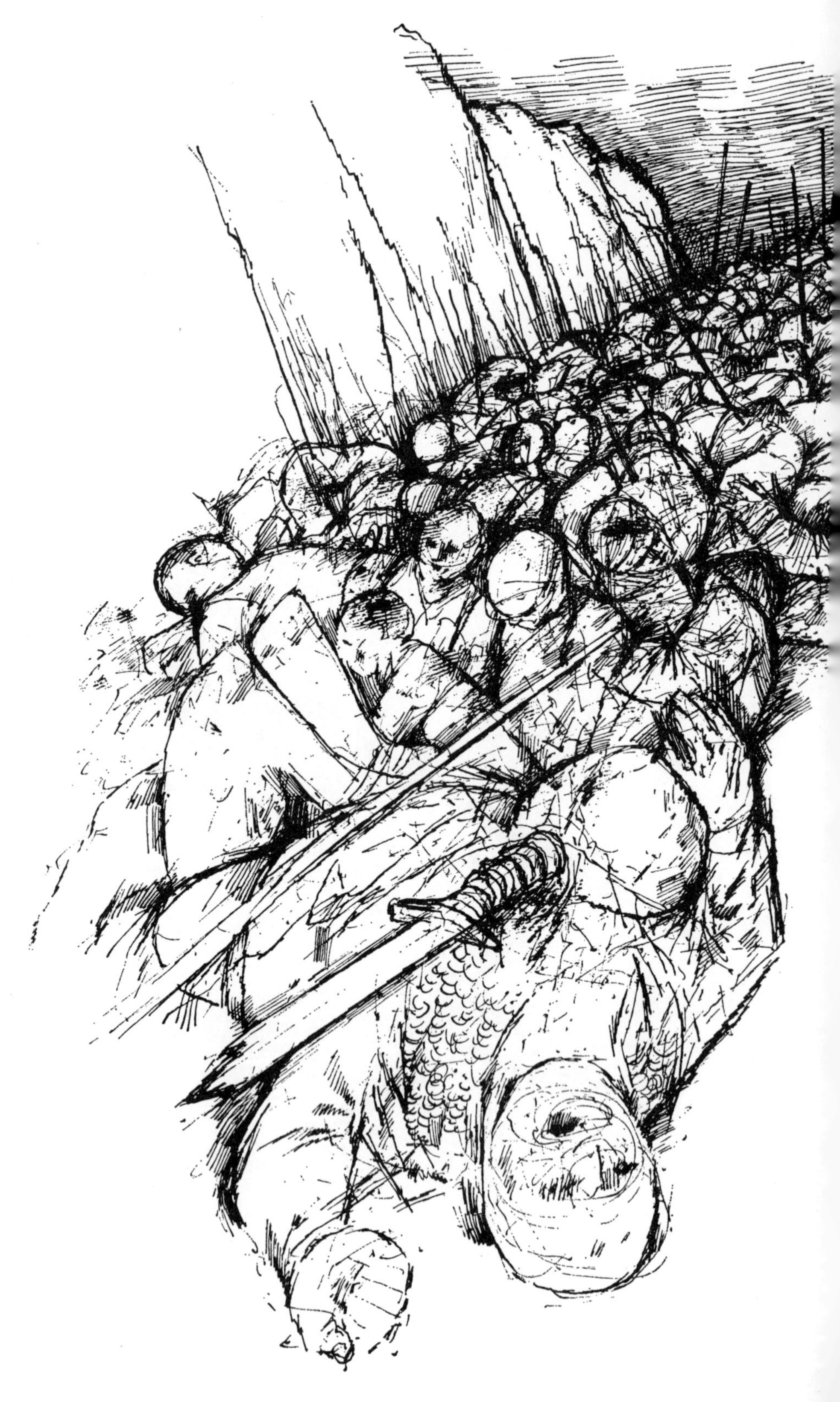

The Battle in the Pass

CHARLEMAGNE, the emperor of the French, had been in Spain for seven years. He had conquered much of it, but some was still under the Moors. They were Mohammedans, who did not worship the Christian god.

One day, Marsilion, king of the Moors, sent Charlemagne a present; lions and bears and greyhounds, seven hundred camels, a thousand falcons and four hundred mules, laden with gold and silver.

"Here are gifts from Marsilion," said his messengers. "If you will return to France, he will follow you there, and swear allegiance to you, and be baptized in the Christian faith."

Charlemagne called a council to discuss what to do.

"It must be a plot. Don't trust him!" exclaimed Charlemagne's nephew, Roland.

"Do what he says," urged Count Ganelon, who was Roland's step-father.

The rest of the nobles agreed that Charlemagne should accept Marsilion's offer.

"Let Ganelon go as our envoy then," shouted Roland furiously.

Charlemagne agreed, and at his command, Ganelon got

ready to go. He was secretly very angry with Roland for having suggested that he should go. He felt he was being treated like a messenger-boy, which was beneath a man of his breeding. So he rode away, beneath the shade of the olive trees, until he caught up with the Moorish envoys. He got into conversation with them.

"You French do harm to everybody," one of the Moors accused him.

"Not all the French, just Roland," said Ganelon, who was still brooding over his grievance. They started talking about Roland, and what harm they could do him.

At last they came to where Marsilion was holding court under a pine tree.

"I bring a message from Charlemagne," said Ganelon, who had been busy planning what lies he could tell. "He insists that you must be baptized as a Christian, and that you must give him half the territory you hold in Spain. Half of it he will give back to you, to administer with him as your overlord, and half of it will go to his nephew Roland. If you don't agree, he will drag you away in fetters to France, and there he will cut off your head."

Marsilion was overwhelmed with fury, and nearly struck Ganelon.

"Wait one moment. Count Ganelon may be able to help us," whispered one of the men who had talked with him on the road.

Marsilion looked cunning, and beckoned Ganelon to him.

"When will Charlemagne weary of fighting?" he asked. "I've heard stories that he's two hundred years old."

"Never as long as Roland and his friend Oliver live," answered Ganelon.

"I have an army of four hundred thousand men. Could they defeat Charlemagne, do you think?"

"Only if you can kill Roland. He is the most powerful of all Charlemagne's men."

"And how could I do that?" asked Marsilion thoughtfully.

"Charlemagne must pass through the Pyrenees to get back to France. Supposing that the main army was to go through, and Roland was to wait until last, with the rear-guard. If you attacked him then, he would not have many men to defend himself with. . . ."

"But someone would have to arrange that Roland was in the rear-guard," Marsilion mused. Then he reached out and gripped Ganelon's hand. "Will you swear to do so yourself?"

So treacherous Ganelon swore to arrange for Roland's death. Marsilion gave him gold and precious jewels, and he went back to Charlemagne.

"Marsilion will do whatever you want," he lied.

Charlemagne and his army set off on the homeward journey to France. They climbed up the steep, rocky Pyrenees until they approached a narrow pass where a winding road led between mountain peaks. The place was called Roncevaux.

"Someone must stay and guard the pass while the main part of the army goes through in safety," said Charlemagne.

"Let Roland," suggested Ganelon.

"But Roland always leads my army," Charlemagne objected.

"I shall do whatever I am asked to do," Roland said proudly, and nobody could persuade him to change his mind.

The French army began to make their way through the pass. It was very narrow, so they had to go in single file. It was very steep, so they had to go slowly. Hour after hour, the long procession went through: the noblemen on their horses, foot-soldiers with their weapons, trails of mules laden with luggage. The clatter of hooves, and the jingle of harness and the clank of their shields could be heard from many miles off. As they emerged at the other side of the pass, they could see their own country of France, spread out, a long way below them. They thought of their wives and families who were waiting for them at home.

High above them, the rear-guard stood on the rocky crags overlooking the pass. They were tensed and alert, waiting to do battle with any one who attacked the main part of the army.

As King Charlemagne rode away from Spain, he hid his face in his cloak to hide the sadness which overwhelmed him.

"What is troubling you?" somebody asked.

"I dreamt that France will be ruined, and that something most dreadful is going to happen to my nephew, Roland."

As he was lamenting, the Moors were getting ready for battle. They armed a great force of four hundred thousand men, led by nobles who were fierce and thirsting for battle. All of them had taken a vow to kill Roland. They armed themselves for the fight in a grove of pine trees. The sunlight filtered down through the leaves, and glinted on their helmets and shields. As they rode forth, their banners streamed out, scarlet and blue and white. They sounded a thousand trumpets, and the triumphant blare reached Roland and his companions, a band of only twenty thousand men.

"The Moors are coming," said Oliver.

"I'll welcome them!" Roland exclaimed. "It is a fine thing for a man to do battle on behalf of his lord. He must endure all hardships of heat or cold, he must suffer whatever is asked of him, and he must be ready to die for his king and for Christ."

While Roland was talking, Oliver had climbed up to a vantage-place to see what was happening. He peered through the narrow end of a ravine, and saw an immense army spread out on the plain below him. Their helmets were glinting with gold and jewels, and their weapons flashed in the sun. He scrambled down in dismay.

"This is the biggest army that's ever been gathered together on earth, and they're ready to fight the fiercest battle that's ever been fought. Roland, sound your horn, and call back the main part of our army."

"I'd be ashamed to," said Roland scornfully. "I'll kill the whole lot of them. My sword will be crimson with heathen blood."

"Roland, sound your horn, and summon King Charlemagne back."

"No one shall ever say that we French were afraid to fight. I'll make those Saracens regret that they ever dared to attack us."

"Roland, I beg you to sound your horn."

"That would bring dishonour upon me. I swear that our enemies will all die."

"There would be no dishonour," protested Oliver. "I have seen the army that's coming against us. It's spread out all over the plain, and up the slopes of the mountains. Compared to it, we have only a handful of men ourselves."

"That makes me thirst for the fight all the more. Remember that what King Charlemagne loves us for is our courage."

As Roland spoke, he became more fierce than a lion or a leopard. Then Archbishop Turpin rode up.

"We must be brave," he called to the troops. "We are fighting for our King and for Christ."

They all knelt down, and he blessed them.

Then Roland rode proudly out to the end of the narrow pass. He held his lance high, and a milk-white pennon streamed out from it. The fringes of the pennon fell over his fingers. He stared at the huge army that was riding up the mountain-side to them.

"Here come the Saracens looking for trouble. We'll capture a fine lot of booty from them."

With a furious battle-cry, the French army rushed downhill in a charge. Then the two armies met. There was a deafening clash of lances against shields, the clatter of armour as wounded men fell from their horses, wild battle-cries, the high-pitched neighs of terrified horses. Lances shattered, shields were cleft in two, keen swords cut through the tightly-ringed coats of mail. The two armies milled around, closely locked together in fight. Oliver was hit by a passing blow which did not wound him. Roland dealt so many tremendous blows with his spear that it splintered to pieces, and he started to lay about him with his bare sword. He cut a pathway right through the Saracens' army. Dead men fell to either side of him, and his horse was covered with streaming blood. Oliver's spear was broken, and he fought with only the stump of the shaft. He was too busy even to draw his sword. The ground was all littered with broken weapons. The banners, which had streamed in the air so bravely, lay scattered, blood-stained and torn.

Meanwhile, in France, Charlemagne looked anxiously up at the mountain barrier between his own country and Spain. He expected to see Roland and the rest of the rear-guard appear at any moment, with their task accomplished. A wind was getting up, and clouds appeared. Soon, the wind started to blow more fiercely, tossing the clouds about, and torrents of rain fell sheer from the sky. The sun was hidden, and the air became darker and darker, until the only light was vivid flashes of lightning, with dense blackness in between. All over France, houses shook because of the force of the storm. Everyone thought that it must be the Day of Judgement. They did not know it was Roland's plight which had called up these terrible portents.

At last, at Roncevaux, the French won the victory. They wandered over the battlefield, seeking among the huge piles of bodies for their friends who were wounded or dead. But as they did so, a still greater army came riding up the mountain towards them. Marsilion himself led them. At a signal, their seven hundred trumpets brayed forth. Roland looked up, startled.

"This is treachery, Oliver. Ganelon, who arranged for us to have stayed here, must have sworn to have us destroyed."

Then the Saracen army appeared. One of them rode out in front. His skin glittered as black as tar, and he flaunted a banner with a fierce dragon on it. Archbishop Turpin rode out to meet him, and dealt him a terrible blow that split him in half. All the French cheered wildly. Then their spirits changed as they saw the army coming towards them. On and on it came, a seemingly endless line. They began to murmur among themselves that they should still run away while there was still time.

"Shame on you," cried the Archbishop. "What does it matter if we all die tonight? Soon we shall all be in Paradise."

Then battle started again. The weapons and the jewelled helmets sparkled, until they were dulled by blood. The two armies hacked and hewed, until the dead lay heaped about in their thousands. Of all the French rear-guard of some twenty thousand, only sixty were left alive.

"What can we do?" gasped Roland. "Let me blow my horn, and summon our king to help us."

Oliver looked at him proudly.

"You disdained to do so before. If you had sounded your horn when I asked you to, we would never have got in this mess. I despise the idea of asking for help now we are desperate."

"Stop quarrelling you two," the Archbishop commanded

sharply. "Charlemagne cannot arrive in time to save us, but at least he can wreak his vengeance on those who are going to slaughter us. And he can give Christian burial to our bodies, not leave us for food for the wolves."

So Roland set the horn to his lips and blew. Nearly a hundred miles away, Charlemagne heard the sound.

"Our men are fighting," he said in a startled voice.

"You must be wrong," Ganelon answered.

Once again, Roland blew, so hard and so painfully that the veins in his temples burst, and blood spurted from his mouth.

"That must be Roland," Charlemagne said again. "He would never blow his horn unless he was fighting."

"You're imagining things. He must be hunting a hare," Ganelon scoffed.

For the last time, Roland blew his horn, and his mouth ran with blood.

"There must be a battle!" the French exclaimed.

They sprang on to their horses and spurred them on, back to the mountains again. They were half angry, half frightened about what was happening to Roland. They rode up the mountain-side, and huge cliffs of rock overshadowed them, and through deep gorge-like valleys, where streams ran swiftly. They sounded their horns in answer to Roland.

Roland himself stood still for one moment. He knew that nearly all his men were already dead. He sighed, then seized his sword again, and fought on. Many Saracens fled, but others surged forward, yelling their battle-cry. They were Ethiopians, with shining black faces and sharp, gnashing white teeth.

"We are doomed," said Roland. "But let us sell our lives dearly. For every one of us who dies, let fifteen heathen be killed."

With that, they renewed the fight. One of the Saracens, on a sorrel horse, rode up to Oliver from behind, and stuck a spear through his back. In agony, Oliver spun round, clutching his sword. He slit straight through the Saracen's head. Then he started to lash around him, hewing the pagans to pieces. Blood streamed from his wound, and fell in pools on the ground, and his face became greyer and greyer. At last, he slumped in the saddle, and Roland gently took off his helmet. Unable to see, Oliver stumbled off his horse. He knelt down, and commended his soul to God. Then he fell to the ground, dead. Roland, his companion for so many years, gazed down at him sadly.

"Now you are dead, I no longer wish to live any longer myself."

For a moment, he nearly fainted in the saddle himself, and only his stirrups kept him from falling.

When he came to, he realized that, of all his men, only himself and two others were left alive. Soon there was only one other man left, the Archbishop. Once more, Roland took up his horn. His head was whirling and racked with pain from the prodigious blasts he had blown. This time, he blew only feebly.

The advancing French army heard the faint note. Charlemagne looked up in dismay.

"Roland is dying. We must hurry to him. Sound the trumpets to let him know we are coming."

The tumult of sixty thousand trumpets reached Roncevaux.

"The French are coming," the Saracens cried. "Quick, let us finish off Roland while we have time. If he lives, he will never cease harrying us."

So Roland and the Archbishop stood side by side to wait for the last assault. Spears and lances flew towards them.

Roland's horse was killed underneath him, but they still fought on, until the Saracens fled.

"We have won," said the Archbishop faintly, for he knew he was dying. He said a prayer over the dead men, and Roland carried Oliver's body to lie beside them. He wept for the death of so many valiant men, and of his closest friend, then he swooned away in his grief. The Archbishop tried to crawl to a stream to fetch him water to drink, but collapsed and died.

Roland was left alone on the field of battle. He dragged himself up to a hill with a sword in one hand and his horn in the other, and gazed out towards Spain, until he, too, sank senseless.

One of the Saracens, who had been feigning death, sprang up as Roland fell. He ran towards him and tried to drag his sword from his hand. Roland stirred, and, clutching his horn, battered the man to death. The mouth of the horn broke into fragments with the force of the blows.

With the last strength he had, Roland dragged himself to his feet, and struck his sword on a stone, again and again and again.

"I fought many battles with you for Charlemagne. You must never fall into heathen hands."

At last, he realized that the sword would not break. He lay down under a pine tree, with his sword and horn hidden beneath him. He turned his face towards Spain, as a conqueror might, and commended his soul to Almighty God.

When Charlemagne and the French reached him, vowing a terrible vengeance, he was lying there, dead.

The Earthly Paradise

Far to the East, where none who sin,
But only righteous men, come in,
These regions stand,
Of flowering woods and fragrant air,
And streams cool as the sea, a fair
And joyous land.

No frost can strike there, no fire blast,
No wild storm rage, nor the sun cast
Too fierce a light.
No winter comes there, no leaves fall,
The fruit hangs ripe and golden, all
The flowers are bright.

There is no distress or weeping,
No disease or slow death creeping
Upon the old.
No wars there, nor any sorrows,
No poor men, who dread tomorrow's
Hunger and cold.

No bleak crags or barren mountains
Or sharp cliffs, but shining fountains
Spring fresh and clean
To water all the blossoming plain
And billowing groves, where trees remain
Eternal green.

Sources

The originals of these stories are mostly anonymous and in many cases the date cannot be determined. They can all be found in modern English translations, sometimes in several different versions. The originals are as follows:

THE FLOOD
in THE EPIC OF GILGAMESH *Babylonian, about 2000 B.C.*

THE FIGHT FOR THE CROWN
in THE CONTENDINGS OF HORUS AND SET *Egyptian, about 1150 B.C.*

WEIGHED IN THE BALANCE
in THE BOOK OF THE DEAD *Egyptian, about 1155–1090 B.C.*

THE SECRET OF KING MINOS
in LIFE OF THESEUS by Plutarch *Greek, lived about A.D. 46 to about A.D. 120*

THE DISGRACEFUL BABY
in the Homeric HYMN TO HERMES *Greek, Author and date unknown*

HOW WINTER CAME TO THE EARTH
in METAMORPHOSES by Ovid *Latin, born 43 B.C. died A.D. 18*

THE FUGITIVE
in THE AENEID by Virgil *Latin, born 70 B.C. died 19 B.C.*

THE UNINVITED GUESTS
in THE ODYSSEY by Homer *Greek, date unknown, possibly ninth century B.C.*

SWIMMING TO SCHOOL
in the NATURAL HISTORY by Pliny the Elder *Latin, born A.D. 23 or 24 died A.D. 79*

HOW THOR FOOLED THE GIANTS
in THE ELDER (OR POETIC) EDDA *Icelandic, possibly between ninth and eleventh centuries*

HOW THE GIANTS FOOLED THOR
in THE YOUNGER (OR PROSE) EDDA by Snorri Sturluson *Icelandic, born 1179 died 1241*

THE TWILIGHT OF THE GODS
in THE YOUNGER EDDA

THE CURSE OF THE DRAGON'S GOLD
in THE SAGA OF THE VOLSUNGS *Icelandic, thirteenth century*

THE WATER MONSTERS
in BEOWULF *English, seventh or eighth century*

THE GIANT'S DAUGHTER
in THE MABINOGION *Welsh, eleventh century or earlier*

SIR GAWAIN AND THE GREEN KNIGHT
in SIR GAWAIN AND THE GREEN KNIGHT *English, fourteenth century*

"IN YOU MY DEATH, IN YOU MY LIFE"
in TRISTAN by Gottfried von Strassburg *German, written about 1200*

THE WEREWOLF
in THE LAYS OF MARIE DE FRANCE *French, twelfth century*

THE BATTLE IN THE PASS
in THE SONG OF ROLAND *French, eleventh century*

THE EARTHLY PARADISE
in THE PHOENIX *English, possibly by Cynewulf, lived in eighth century, based on a Latin poem by Lactantius, lived about 250–317*